# LIVING ALONE—A WOMAN'S GUIDE

LIZ MCNEILL TAYLOR is a freelance journalist. She is the author of a number of books, and has written articles for a variety of magazines including *Woman*, *Woman's Realm* and *Good Housekeeping*. She spent ten years living with her husband in India, but in her forties she was widowed and brought up her four children on her own. She now lives alone in Scotland.

GW00659986

# Overcoming Common Problems

A successful and popular series to give you practical
help for the emotional and medical problems of
everyday life.

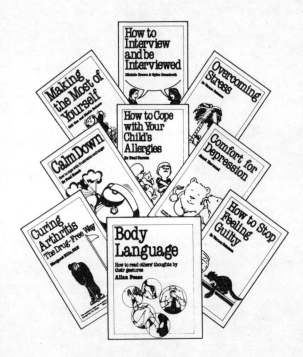

Paperbacks £1·95 to £4·95
Available from all good bookshops

 *For a complete list of titles write to;*
Sheldon Press Mail Order,
SPCK, Marylebone Road, London NW1 4DU

Overcoming Common Problems

# LIVING ALONE – A WOMAN'S GUIDE

*Liz McNeill Taylor*

SHELDON PRESS
LONDON

First published in Great Britain in 1987 by
Sheldon Press, SPCK, Marylebone Road, London NW1 4DU

Second impression 1988

British Library Cataloguing in Publication Data

Taylor, Liz McNeill
    Living alone : a woman's guide————
    Overcoming Common Problems
    1. Single women————Conduct of life
    2. Living alone
    I. Title II. Series
    306.8'8        HQ800.2

ISBN 0–85969–539–5
ISBN 0–85969–540–9 Pbk

Typeset by WBC Print Ltd, Bristol
Printed in Great Britain by
Richard Clay Ltd, Bungay, Suffolk

# Contents

# Introduction

To live alone does not mean to be lonely. To live alone does not mean to be dissatisfied with life. To live alone does not mean to be isolated or afraid. Living alone can in fact be a very satisfying and secure way of life; for many people it can be a liberation.

This feeling of liberation comes from the knowledge that there is no-one else in your life to annoy or supervise you unless you choose to invite them to do so. The noise and clutter of a constantly shared life and the feeling of being observed all the time are avoided. The spice of freedom and independence heightens the pleasure of a single existence, and leads to enhanced self-awareness and enjoyment of life.

Only a generation ago it was considered shameful to admit to living alone. It was thought that people who preferred living on their own to living with someone else were peculiar, withdrawn and in danger of having an unhealthy lifestyle.

Today, however, more people live on their own than at any time since social records were kept and the old fashioned view of single living as an aberration or a social misery has had to be radically changed.

This has come about because the number of people who choose to live alone has been steadily rising since the 1950s. In the national population census returns for Great Britain in 1982 one of the findings was that 23 per cent of households were single person homes. Since then the graph has gone on rising and today the figure is 25 per cent. It was calculated in 1983 that over 9 per cent of the total population of the United Kingdom were living in either privately owned or rented accommodation which means that over six million people in Great Britain live alone. In the United States of America the proportion is even higher, running today at almost 11 per cent, and most of these

1

people live in cities or in older people's condominiums which were first built in America but are now being built all over Europe and Britain. As people become more mobile and the ties of family gradually loosen, the trend towards single person living is growing in the Western world.

The majority of people living on their own are women. It has been estimated that three quarters of the occupants of single person homes in Britain are female and they are also predominantly in the older age groups because 57 per cent of them are aged 75 or over. This is partly explained by the longevity of the female as opposed to the male, for many one person units contain widows.

For both sexes, however, the possibility of living alone increases with age, and statistics published by the Central Statistical Office in 1986 show that in the mid 1980s just over a half of all people aged 75 and over lived alone. This figure had risen from one sixth of the over-75 population since 1973. It can be partly explained by medical advances which allow people to stay independent longer and partly because of the increased number of people who have become owner-occupiers over the past two decades. People who own their own homes are not so likely to move into institutions as they grow older.

Those in younger age groups are not so likely to be living alone. The proportion of single home occupancy rises with age; in the 50 to 64 age group 9.3 per cent live alone but those in the 19 to 25 group are not unexpectedly much less likely to be living on their own. Only 0.9 per cent of people under 24 live alone in their own homes, but this figure gives a false impression because it does not take account of the very large proportion of single young people who live in rented accommodation. The trend towards single living however has increased even in younger groups because the official figures also show that the percentage of people living alone doubled between 1973 and 1984 for both the group aged between 25 and 44 and the group between 16 and 24. Single living is spreading fast.

At any time in Britain there are around six million people living alone. Are they all miserable? Are they all lonely? The answer is most definitely 'no'. The significance of the growing number of single person homes is not, as some commentators would have us believe, a sad reflection on the disruption of modern life. It is not a sign that the Western world is slipping into a state of mass paranoia and crippling loneliness. Instead it could be a sign that more and more people are learning to value their independence, to rely on their own resources, to be their own people.

It would be false to deny that feelings of misery and loneliness can strike even the most independent single people, but there are times when everyone feels lonely, even those living in close families. Something can be done about loneliness and it is not a necessary accompaniment to living on your own. More seriously, there are of course many sad and isolated people tucked away in the official figures for single person living, who are unable or unwilling to recognize that something can be done about loneliness, and these feelings can take over their lives. The problem of loneliness for solitary people should not be denied, but it can and must be faced if the advantages of living alone are to be fully realized.

Those who come to relish their own company find that there are aspects to life which had previously gone unnoticed or unappreciated. By learning to be happy alone you have a greater chance of learning to integrate with others more successfully when you do into the world. The discovery that it is possible to have an identity and an enjoyment of life entirely without the appreciation and support of other people is life enhancing.

The feeling of liberation that being on your own brings, the knowledge that no-one is around to annoy or supervize you, adds a spice to single existence. The noise and clutter of having someone else always around, the feeling of being always observed, is part of shared living that those who live alone do not have to suffer.

The purpose of this book is to provide affirmation, advice and support for those who want to live alone and like it.

*How it happened to me*
Like many other people, when I was young I didn't really consider the prospect of living alone—and liking it. I am

intensely gregarious and having my husband and children around me gave me intense pleasure, so the prospect of living on my own in a cottage with my dogs and cats made me shiver with dread—until I started to do it.

I was totally alone for the first time in my life on the day that my youngest child went off to boarding school. I had been a widow for several years by that time but I had never been socially isolated or alone—having four children at home had made sure of that. However eventually the three oldest went off into the world and on that sunny autumn afternoon as I sat on the stairs, I listened to the clocks ticking loudly away all over the house.

I had never consciously heard the noise they made before and it struck me that after a life of noise and bustle I was going to be left alone with only the clocks for company. The prospect seemed so appalling that I wept.

However it did not take long before the positive aspects of living alone began to present themselves to me. I found a new delight in coming and going as I pleased: I could live my life according to my own rules, eat what I liked when I liked, play the radio all night if I chose without worrying whether the things I was doing were disturbing someone else. There was no clutter in the house that was not of my making; there was no noise. I discovered that living alone is a very pleasant way of life.

Today I am a happy solitary and I have found that creative solitude can be used in a building and enforcing way. I am alone but I am very far from being lonely.

# ONE

# Living Alone From Choice and Circumstance

Many people who live alone do so from choice. They are happier on their own than they would ever be with a permanent companion. They find there are things about life which can only be fully appreciated alone. Periods of withdrawal are of paramount importance for people who find that constant togetherness, even with those they love dearly, becomes wearing.

Very often when we fear the prospect of being on our own it is because we are reacting in the way we have been conditioned. The popular idea of someone who lives alone through choice is of the 'loner', the hermit, the oddity and misfit in normal social relationships. Solitaries through choice are regarded with pity and also sometimes with distrust. The fact however is that some of us are not temperamentally suited to a shared life.

Although modern thinking still reveres the 'family' as the ideal social unit, it should be recognized that there are other ways of living which can be as good or better for certain individuals.

Psychiatrists in fact often claim that many sufferers from mental illnesses and breakdowns are only pinpointing the confusions and frustrations of the collective of family members with whom they live. The psychiatrists recognize they should not just be treating one individual but the entire family because the patient is a focal point for the disturbances of spouses, parents or siblings.

Many people start out living alone as a gesture of independence. They move away from home and establish themselves happily alone in a flat or a bed sitter as soon as they can—not always because they are unhappy at home but more often because they want to live their own lives, free and without supervision. Because they achieve this, it is then possible for them to maintain a better relationship with the family they have left behind.

It should be recognized that there are people who prefer their own company for a large part of the time. Perhaps they have grown up as only children, accustomed to amusing themselves. Perhaps they lead an engrossing interior life that requires no other person to make it satisfying. This is not a sign of peculiarity, but should be recognized as a perfectly normal personality type. Very often people who are introverted when young grow into better integrated and happy people in adulthood and middle age than those who were very gregarious, who 'led the pack' and were excessively extraverted.

There is no need to feel guilty about preferring to live alone, it is not a sign of gross selfishness. Freely acknowledge what it is you want from life, accept your own needs and recognize that it is not self indulgent to pursue them. If you are the sort of person who thrives on being alone, you will only be denying a part of yourself if you ignore your own nature.

If you are one of the people for whom regular periods of withdrawal are beneficial, like a child going into a satisfying Wonderland, you will relish the ability to shut your door and be alone—not lonely, not isolated but happily *alone*.

### The value of solitude

Some people live alone because it is not possible for them to work in close proximity with others—artists, musicians and writers find creative solitude can be used in a constructive way. They cannot concentrate on their work while their attention is distracted or while outside demands are being made on them. It is essential to be able to think alone without distraction and they usually find they have to shut themselves away from other people for the entire period of creation. The thriller writer Georges Simenon used to shut himself up in solitude for six weeks at a time while he was writing his novels.

Literary pilgrimages are often paid to the solitary work places of artists, poets and authors—Dylan Thomas'

Laugharne boathouse is one of them—and the memoirs of many other writers are full of references to their need to be alone. Very few have been like Jane Austen who had the ability to write in a drawing room full of chattering friends and family.

Other cultures and races do not share the Western fear of, and prejudice against, being alone. In fact some of them positively foster the practice of withdrawing from society, of giving the individual valuable times of apartness in life.

Hindus use periods of isolation as a means of spiritual regeneration and during the penultimate stages of life they believe the ideal is to be alone and contemplative, to use the time for formulating a personal philosophy and acceptance of death. They deplore the continual modern lemming-like rush from place to place which does not allow time for withdrawal and contemplation. If you are always in a hurry to catch the next party or the next plane, you might never have time to catch up with yourself.

In some aboriginal tribes adolescent males have to spend a period of time away from all the others in order to achieve some knowledge of themselves and to 'grow up' into men.

The spiritual value of retreat is recognized in western society as well. Monks and nuns in religious orders know the value of the spirit of isolation. They know that by living apart from the rest of the world, they can achieve that tranquillity and acceptance which only comes through deep thought and separation from day-to-day life.

Even animals seem to recognize the value of times of isolation, for if an animal is ill it will drag itself off to some secret, hidden place until it either dies or recovers. The most pampered pet reverts to this primeval need and one of my own dogs, while recovering from an operation, refused to leave the front seat of my son's abandoned Mini, well away from the house and all its distractions. For three days I carried the dog's food out to the car and laid it on the seat beside him. He lay alone concentrating on gathering his strength and when he felt better he came into the house wagging his tail. Being alone had been part of his cure.

As well as those who live alone by choice there are many

people, especially among older groups, who find themselves translated from a shared life to living alone.

### Widowed or divorced
The main reasons for this are widowhood and divorce.

'Forsaking all others' is part of the marriage service which unfortunately should not be taken too literally. The couple who are all in all to each other may be perfect characters for a romantic story but in real life, at least one of them is heading for emotional chaos.

Even if they survive the shoals of marital disagreements, separation and divorce, as Somerset Maugham said of lovers, 'one of them must die before the other'.

Loneliness is the most crippling after effect of widowhood and divorce. Grief softens with time, memories become less painful but loneliness can be a very real problem for someone who has lost the person in whom they placed all their love, all their confidence and all their reliance.

When my husband died I found I had to accept that the fear of loneliness was making my grief worse. When I came to terms with it I realized that time does heal because it teaches us to stand on our own feet. It shows us that we do have the inner resources to stand alone in the world even though our first reactions may be sheer terror at the thought of having to survive in a jungle full of dangers.

It is a hard thing to admit but many widowed people, even those who were very happily married, find that once they have accepted the need to go on alone they discover an entirely new dimension to life.

'After my husband died I made new friends and did things which I would never have done if he'd gone on living. I also discovered things about myself which I wouldn't have had to bring out if I'd continued as a happy wife. I became different and sometimes I think if he was to come back to life, he'd no longer recognize me as the same person. It's a sad thing to have to say but by dying he opened a new world for me. I feel as if I've had the chance to live two lives in the space of one,' said a widow who made a new career for herself after the death of her husband.

The traumas associated with widowhood inflict themselves on the divorced and separated as well. Today one marriage in three ends in divorce and those breakups inevitably cause casualties. The problems of having to cope alone are often exacerbated by feelings of bitterness and loss of self-regard.

*The 'empty nest syndrome'*
When children leave home, behind them they may be leaving a parent who finds an independent existence as unfamiliar as any teenager alone in the city. This can be a crisis time during which the trap of loneliness or unhappy resignation can claim its victim.

Single parents are most prone to this feeling of uselessness which has been called the empty nest syndrome, a graphic description of the feeling that overwhelms one after the children who have been companions and responsibility for so many years, go away. When it happened to me the rest of my life spread in front of me like an empty desert. No-one needed me any longer. What reason was there for going on living?

However, I knew that it would be unfair and over-demanding to attempt to keep my children at home for my sake and I soon realized that a very good reason for going on living was that I was being given a chance to develop a new life.

It is essential to seize the opportunity for doing new things, going to new places, meeting new people, perhaps even starting a new career when your children leave home. No longer is all your money, emotion and interest concentrated on them. You are as free, perhaps even freer, as you have ever been in your life and it would be a great mistake to let the opportunity slip by.

So if the empty nest syndrome threatens to engulf you, avoid the tendency to slip into indifference and inertia. Stiffen your resolve with the sobering thought that there may only be a few years of activity left for you. Get out and make things happen. Finding a new lease of life after children leave home is not disloyal or indifferent. It is better for you and for your children to know that you have banished the need to rely on them for company and can in future be treated as an interesting individual in your own right—not just as mum or dad.

When a parent blossoms into a new career or a new phase of life, children will be able to come back for visits because of love and not just out of duty. They will call up on the telephone with the question, 'What's new?' and know they will receive an interesting reply, not a litany of sighs and woes. Sometimes the reincarnation of the parent takes the children by surprise—they did not realize he or she had it in them to branch out on their own with such panache.

Children should not leave home with the extra burden of a demanding mother or father weighing them down from a distance. It may be necessary to be firm with both yourself and with them in order to make sure that this does not happen and a widow whose children grew up and left, sent the last one off with the Spartan-sounding injunction;

'If you come back home to see me because you think you should and not because you really want to, I'll slam the door in your face!'

### Carers

The death of parents is another time when loneliness can get the upper hand. This happens most frequently when the child is an adult who has lived with the parent, perhaps until the child is middle aged. There may have been times when the relationship was strained but when the parent finally dies, the child who has taken on the role of carer and protector, experiences an unexpected crisis.

Life no longer seems worth living and even the annoyances and strictures that the care of the parent imposed are regretted and longed for. Guilt at past irritation, at things said and now regretted, plays a large part in the sadness and suffering the child endures.

Single women who have stayed at home to look after a parent, often have missed the opportunity of marriage and their only friends are of their parents' generation. Too strangling a bond has been built up between parent and child and when this is broken the upheaval can be traumatically painful.

Always remember that no matter how much you love

your parent and no matter how much they demand of your time, it is a grievous mistake not to build and maintain an outside life for yourself. Some people solve the problem by living close by, but not with, a dependent parent until such time as frailty makes this arrangement no longer possible. Others insist on having time to themselves, entertaining their own friends and establishing a routine of going out without having to explain every time where they are going and when they will be back.

This can be difficult when the parent insists on regarding the child that is in fact looking after them as dependent still but it is up to the child to fight for self identity. Start establishing your own personality as soon as possible in the parent-child relationship and encourage your parent to foster their own independent friendships in which you take little or no part.

Invite your parent's friends round to see them—and then go out yourself. Arrange a 'parent-sitter' for your evenings out if this is necessary. Take a holiday on your own for this is necessary to clear the air between two people living in overclose and sometimes resentful proximity. There are organizations which will arrange for an invalid parent to go into a home or a hospital to allow this to happen. (See Lifestyle appendix for details of day and short-stay relief care.) If both parent and child appreciate the need to lead their own lives, and if the child is able to do this without feeling guilty and selfish, when the parent dies, the child will not be racked with remorse and completely isolated.

For everyone going through times of crisis in which they have to make decisions that can affect the rest of their lives, it is important to realize that there can be beneficial effects from being alone. Not all the world exists in couples and single living is not a sentence of solitude and deprivation.

Being alone for a period of time helps bring your life into focus, helps you to sort out your priorities. Many people then find that it is not essential for them to live life through someone else or to rely entirely on a partner for their sense of identity. Everyone can be an independent unit providing they are prepared to truly examine what it is they want from life and know that they may have to work hard to get it.

# TWO

# Possible Pitfalls

Despite all the benefits of solitude there are particular problems associated with living alone. If you find yourself facing these problems it is important to remember that other people have felt the same way, but also that there are many positive and practical steps you can take to get full benefit from your life alone.

As I have mentioned, loneliness and the fear of loneliness are two major problems which afflict those who live alone, and related to these are dangerous feelings and habits which you should not allow to swamp your enjoyment of life.

It is a sad fact of life that these pitfalls are especially real for women living alone. Men are not as conditioned as women into thinking it is socially essential for them to have a companion in life. They can go out to parties or to pubs on their own and make contacts without being regarded with disapproval or suspicion. It is easier for a man to exist alone than it is for a woman—women need more determination.

## Alcohol and tranquillizers

Sometimes those who live alone develop a vague feeling of being out of tune with life which drives them to consult their doctors with a range of physical symptoms. As has been already said many doctors think that a high ratio of the people they see in their consulting rooms are really protesting against feelings of isolation and this is not always confined to people who live on their own. One woman in five in Britain is taking tranquillizers and young to middle-aged married women are the heaviest users. In 1985 over 40 million prescriptions for tranquillizers were written out by Britain's G.P.s and two-thirds of those prescriptions were given to women. Though the dangers of patients becoming addicted to tranquillizers are now more recognized and most doctors are reluctant to prescribe them for prolonged periods, little counselling is being provided in place of the misleadingly named 'happiness' pill.

It is only too easy for a harried doctor to write out a prescription for a tranquillizer but although it may muffle the suffering it will not cure what ails the patient. Anyone who has ever taken them knows they cannot miraculously change your life. You only feel smothered, as if you had lost your vital force, but the troubles you had before you took the tranquillizer are still with you—there is no magical cure by popping a pill into your mouth.

Change and improvement in the way the sufferer feels can only be brought about by doing something—by changing outlook, way of life and expectations. If you think about asking a doctor for a tranquillizer try to take a cool, analytical look at what has gone wrong with your life instead. If there is any clear headed, honest and uninvolved friend whom you can discuss this with, that will be even better. Unfortunately most general practitioners do not have the time to investigate what a distressed patient really needs. Even when psychiatric counselling is given, the final solution ultimately lies in the hands of the sufferers themselves. There are cases and times when the solution seems drastic and demands seeing yourself in an unflattering light but if you think about your problems long and deep enough, a solution or a reconciliation with things which you have been warring against will inevitably appear.

The same sadness and the same problems that drive people to tranquillizers can persuade them to forget their troubles in alcohol. Alcoholism used to be mainly a male problem but in the last decade the number of women heavy drinkers has been rising steadily. It has now reached the stage where the woman alcoholic is recognized as a special problem in her own right. What is generally unrecognized by women when they begin drinking is that it takes far less to turn them into alcoholics than it does for men—in fact a woman's alcohol level is a third lower than a man's. King's College Hospital in London has a Liver Unit which warns that a woman can develop cirrhosis of the liver if her daily alcohol intake exceeds forty grams of alcohol a day. Forty grams of alcohol is equivalent to two double measures of spirits or four glasses of wine.

Because women are also more adept at covering up the traces of their addiction, it takes longer for their problem to be discovered. They are usually in an acute stage before families and friends recognize what is happening. Many women secret drinkers say they started by having a 'sustaining' sherry in the afternoon or evening because they felt lonely and the drink cheered them up.

'It made me look on the bright side, it gave me a different outlook. Soon it became a habit for me to have a sherry as soon as I got into the house from work. I'd reach for the bottle before I made myself a cup of tea. By nine o'clock I was drunk and usually staggered off to bed. When I realized what I was doing I went to my doctor and fortunately he arranged for me to get help,' said one woman whose growing addiction was arrested in time.

Alcoholism is not, of course, only a female problem— many men are also badly affected by it, but there is now a wider recognition of it being a disease more than a sign of character weakness and doctors are more alert to the dangers of even a moderate intake of alcohol. In many medical practices doctors are routinely questioning patients about their alcohol intake in much the same way as they take blood pressure readings. By doing this they frequently uncover cases of incipient alcoholism which can then be stopped in time. Too often the people involved do not realize that they are on the edge of becoming problem drinkers. They imagine that their intake is normal and they feel that their 'little drink' has a therapeutic, not a harmful, effect on them. Once they are alerted to the true danger and realize why drink helps them, they can often sort out the hidden problem in their lives that they are drinking to forget.

There are clinics and charities in Britain which run alcohol withdrawal programmes but the oldest and most widely established is the famous organization Alcoholics Anonymous which has helped so many people live normal lives again after the nightmare of drink addiction. A.A.

operates worldwide and it concentrates on the 'day at a time' programme which guides drinkers through the stage when to lapse back into drinking is an ever present temptation. There are also several others that can help people with an alcohol problem, either incipient or actual and two of these are Accept and Alcohol Concern—their addresses are in the appendix. They all insist however that the only people who can really change the habits of alcoholics are the sufferers themselves.

## Eating problems

Loneliness and desperation drive people to strange and self-destructive ways of solacing themselves. Many people gorge on food, seeking comfort on a plate, or fail to feed themselves properly.

A sense of isolation drives some to the refrigerator or the corner sweet shop. Satisfying the yearning for sweet things, and especially for chocolate, makes them feel cherished and comforted like a child rewarded for being good. In fact chocolate contains chemicals that soothe the mind and calm hidden desires but the problem is that it also puts fat on the people who eat too much of it. When feeling low, the temptation to wolf a bar of chocolate is almost irresistible. Yield by all means, because it is not necessary to become a total prohibitionist about your pleasures—but not too often.

The most difficult time for people living alone is usually the evening. At adroitly chosen times, television advertisements offer tempting looking drinks or snack foods, hoping to make your mouth water and overcome a determination not to eat. It helps to realize that the psychologists who advise advertisers know the times when captive viewers are at their most susceptible. By resisting their blandishments you can feel you have won a sort of victory.

Excess weight is as big a health hazard as addiction to drink or drugs. Diseases of the heart, the kidneys and diabetes dog the overweight. When I was a student studying history at university, our professor described Emperor Charles V as having 'dug his own grave with his teeth'. I have never forgotten that evocative phrase which haunts me when my own weight rises above an acceptable level today.

The problem is that eating for comfort is an insidious habit. When you live alone there is no-one who can point out to you the early signs of putting on weight. Usually by the time you wake up to it yourself, the damage is already done and you are doomed to the penance of slimming or, if that effort seems too much, to a constant see-sawing between eating and starving.

It is a good idea to set a regular routine for yourself and step on the bathroom scales every morning. They never tell lies or give flattering replies, and when the needle goes up too high, get an exercise bike, go swimming, jogging or join a slimming class. A friend also with a tendency to gain weight keeps a chart in the back of the bathroom door, and plots the graph of his weight day by day. This is both a sort of game and a regulation for him. Above all, no matter what methods of conscience prompting you use, stay away from the tempting fridge or the hidden biscuit box.

The other danger comes when people on their own gradually lose interest in food and neglect their nutrition. They may cut vegetables out of their diet because they do not particularly like them; they avoid fruit and, forgetting about vitamins, stick to fast foods until they harm their health.

### Healthy eating

Vitamins are essential not only for good health but for a good frame of mind. You feel more able to cope with life, more optimistic and more competent if your nutritional intake is correctly balanced. Vitamin A helps the skin and the eyes; vitamin B is essential for general health; vitamin C prevents colds and flu; vitamin D is the 'sunshine' vitamin and is essential for those living in dull climates and vitamin F, which has recently been more widely recognized and which is found in the oil of the evening primrose, maintains hormonal balance. To keep fit take a multi-vitamin tablet every day.

Also try to ensure that you balance your food intake,

adding fibre, green vegetables and fresh fruit even though you may not particularly like any of those things. It is as dangerous to become indifferent or uncaring about food as it is to be overfond of it.

A woman who decided there was no point cooking for herself, restricted herself to eating everything out of tins. Even her breakfast grapefruit was tinned, so were her potatoes, her vegetables and her puddings. After ten years of eating like this, she developed liver cancer and died though she never drank alcohol.

It is not necessary on grounds of avoiding unnecessary expense to restrict your diet to small tins or packets of processed foods for people on their own can now buy single portions of most fresh foods in supermarkets and particularly in Marks and Spencer's who sell one-person portions of their delicious specialist dishes. No longer do food shops turn up their noses at the customer who asks for a very small piece of cheese or only two slices of ham.

The awareness of the potentially huge market among people living alone was seen by Delia Smith, the cookery writer, whose 'Cooking for One' T.V. programme and later book, *One is Fun*, were an immense success. When she first suggested the idea the television bosses doubted if there would be a big enough interest in it from the public but her hunch proved to be right—there are thousands of people who want to find out how to cook satisfying and interesting meals for themselves.

Delia Smith's series showed that it is not self indulgent to make sure that the food you cook for yourself is both nutritious and interesting. Taking the time and trouble to prepare a tasty and attractive looking meal can add interest and practical benefits to your life. It is not gluttony, it is common sense. And although everyone should be aware of the dangers of alcoholism that does not mean a total ban on alcohol. A glass of wine with your meal is good for you.

## Sexual starvation

One of the root causes of unhappiness among many people living on their own is the lack of a sexual companion. This is rarely openly admitted but is clothed in romantic or allusive terms . . . 'I'd like a companion, someone to be with me, someone to love.'

The problem is exacerbated by the fact that society sees people as in some way insufficient if they are not half of a couple. You feel, and society feels, that there is something wrong with you if there is not a lover in your life.

However it is perfectly possible to live happily and healthily as a celibate in spite of a lot of theories about mental problems being caused by lack of sex. Thousands of men and women manage to live perfectly integrated and happy lives without it on a regular basis.

There are people however who feel the need for sex with painful intensity and unless they are prepared to be casually promiscuous—which is now seen as being more dangerous to health than abstinence—there is often very little they can do about it. Another problem about casual promiscuity is that it causes more emotional upsets than it eases because of the feeling of disappointment and disillusion when affairs come to an end. The man or woman who 'sleeps around' ends up more lonely and unhappy than those who settle down to living without sex at all.

## Psychological problems

It is common for those who develop a solitary lifestyle to foster minor peculiarities which may never drive them to a doctor but which can limit their lives and ultimately cause isolation. These often result from a lack of perspective on life and outside interests.

Agoraphobia and anxiety neuroses are examples of this, for anyone who lives too withdrawn a life can very easily find it first difficult, and perhaps later impossible, to go out and face the world which comes to seem hostile and dangerous. Terror of crowds, of busy shops, even of social gatherings can severely restrict the lives of those who are overtaken by such fears. Their solution is to avoid situations which give rise to their fear but gradually even the act of stepping over their own front door becomes too much for them. Any disruption of their routine disturbs them deeply. An understanding friend who can support a sufferer through the trauma of going out is essential if any recovery is to be made.

*Hypochondria*
People who have nothing else but themselves to think about begin to monitor themselves too closely. Every ache, every pain, every gasp for breath becomes a cause of concern which can grow into a fixation if there is no-one in whom they can confide, no-one who can laugh their fears away if they are unfounded or else urge them to go to a doctor if they seem serious.

The over-anxious patient is always in and out of the doctor's surgery complaining of vague symptoms. One problem is that when and if they do become ill, their doctor can often disregard the complaint as being just another of their fancies.

The most serious kind of hypochondriac however is the one who will not go to a doctor at all but stays at home nursing their worries, sometimes until they *do* become ill. They live in a continual misery of illness, hedged round with the terrors of dying long before it happens. They are crippled and restrained from normal life by their fears which they irrationally refuse to have either confirmed or proved incorrect. If you find that you watch yourself as closely and as tenderly as a mother watching her first born, get out into the world and do something that occupies your mind sufficiently to make you forget yourself.

Do not brood on your own illnesses, real or imaginary. Worrying about being ill might even make you develop the disease you are worrying about—and that is a real concern for the fully fledged hypochondriac.

It is very easy to start worrying about your own health, to spend hours agonizing over what will happen if you become ill and imagining the time when you are no longer able to look after yourself, before it ever happens. This is a dangerous and unnecessary self indulgence. You should never cross your bridges, especially dangerous bridges, before you come to them.

These problems can become so serious that they lead to

nervous breakdown or major psychological traumas. The risk of this is higher for women than it is for men, as figures for admissions to mental hospitals show. Women are also more likely than men to be readmitted for further treatment, often because they are released to the same life and circumstances that caused their problems in the first place. However, nervous breakdown and the need for specialist treatment are an extreme reaction to unhappiness which of course is not just brought on by living alone or being lonely.

All sorts of fads and fancies adopted by those living alone can also develop into phobias if they are never examined in the cold light of reality. Fixations about security or about infringements of your privacy should not be allowed to dominate life. For example the fear of 'spying neighbours' can become obsessional or the eating of a limited range of foods can gradually be accepted as the only possible way to live if there is no-one else living with you to shake you out of the habit.

Thurber has a story about his aunt who was terrified of electricity because she thought that when she switched on a light dangerous emanations came from the bulb and it has a grounding in truth. She was suffering from a hysterical fancy.

The development of fads is something that can happen very easily to the most stable people who live alone. The discarding of a paper bag can drive one friend of mine into a frenzy against waste. This urge to conserve is admirable in small degrees but a perfectly sane old man who used to live near me saved paper until it was impossible to climb the stairs of his cottage—they were blocked solid with tied up bundles of newspaper. When he died it took workmen weeks to clear out all the carefully hoarded rubbish.

There is however nothing wrong in allowing yourself to be a little eccentric if you live alone. There is great freedom about having no-one to please but yourself and when you cast off constraints that tie you down when with others, an added dimension and pleasure is brought to life. It is a self indulgence which is very liberating. When you get used to doing your own thing, you forget any fears you may once have had about being thought a 'crank' providing your way of life is not too bizarre.

Because there is no-one but yourself to please, you can wear what you like, get up and have a bath at one a.m., work all night and sleep all day if the fancy takes you. Who cares if someone else would think it odd to play the radio all night long? You don't have to explain that it makes you fall asleep. The soothing sound of the World Service lulls me to sleep in the early hours of the morning. I wouldn't be able to have it playing at my ear if there was anyone else in the room.

Who cares if it is not entirely conventional to wear unusual clothes or mix them up to suit your own convenience. Track shoes and a fur coat may look unsuitable to the smartly dressed executive wife next to you in the supermarket checkout—but who cares? I knew an old lady who wandered around in a moleskin coat and a cotton sunbonnet summer and winter. Although she was extremely sane, her neighbours regarded her with great awe and caution—but she didn't care a fig. She enjoyed her reputation for oddness and took great pleasure in occasionally surprising her detractors by going out dressed like a fashion plate.

Making yourself look smart now and again however, even though you normally wear the first and most comfortable thing that comes to hand in the wardrobe, repays the trouble involved both for your own morale and for your standing with other people.

I have always been partial to wearing trousers and did not realize how they swamped my wardrobe until one day, when I was dressed up for a business meeting, I happened to meet my daily on the street. She was about to walk past me without any sign of recognition until I spoke to her. Then she did a double take and said in surprise; 'Oh, it's you. I didn't recognize you without your trousers.'

When I returned home I threw out half of the old pairs of baggy trousers that I had been wearing for years and bought myself some dresses. It was a salutary lesson.

# THREE

# Beating Isolation

Most of the possible pitfalls dealt with in the previous chapter have their roots in loneliness, so it is obviously essential to avoid becoming isolated in order to make the most of life alone.

Many people who find themselves lonely after being widowed or divorced find the thought of going out and making friends again fairly daunting. With practice and determination, however, it will become easier, and there are various techniques and ground-rules which will help you build your confidence.

## Friendship

Friendship is the most undervalued human relationship. To say someone is 'just a friend' is to underestimate seriously their contribution to your wellbeing. Having friends is like having an extra dimension to life.

To make friends it is essential to respect the privacy and importance of every one you meet. You will not become bosom friends with all of them by any means—nor would you want to—but you will be open to developing friendship and from time to time, as you look back on what has happened between you and other people, you will be genuinely surprised.

People warm towards someone who is interested in them, who really wants to listen to what they have to say.

Working as a journalist I have interviewed hundreds of people and long ago discovered that there is a special technique for making even a reluctant and withdrawn interviewee talk. You start by asking them fairly innocuous questions, gently at first and gradually getting more to the point or more personal. It is like tiptoeing through a minefield for you are awake to every nuance of the other person's reactions, physical as well as spoken.

It always interests me how people respond—practically everyone likes talking about themselves. It is not an accusation to say that we are all our own favourite subjects. Given the opportunity to talk about themselves, all but the most extremely hostile and withdrawn subject will expand and expound.

Dorothy Jerrome, a researcher into problems of loneliness and isolation working at Sussex University in a district where there is a high proportion of old and retired people among the population, discovered that the happiest people in that older age group did not rely on their families for companionship—they relied on their friends. Those who made the effort to establish friends, even at fairly advanced ages, were far happier than those who said 'I've got my family, that's enough for me'.

'The Tremendous Ten' was the nickname she gave to a group of ten middle class widows she found in Hastings. They had come together in an informal social club and their mutual friendship was more important to them than their family relationships. They met socially, supported each other, looked after each other when they were sick, went on holiday together and shared their problems. The important thing was this was done in a feeling of equality, they did not feel they were being patronized by younger people or made to feel failing and incapable of handling their own lives as can happen when the elderly rely entirely on their children or grandchildren.

What Dorothy Jerrome found remarkable about 'The Tremendous Ten' was that they had no snobbishness in their friendship and no feelings of 'one-up-man-ship'. There were two subjects which were taboo in their conversations—age and money. Instinctively they refused to allow either of these to give members extra status or a more lowly position in the group.

The true friend is prepared to reach out to people from all walks of life and all ages—children to ninety year olds. What they look for is the inner person that they can appreciate and enjoy. One of the first rules for friendship is to be sincere and uncritical. You must really want to get to know that person; you must not be dismissing them for a private prejudice because if you are secretly hostile or over-critical that will come through to them like an undercurrent. Everyone knows the feeling of 'What does that person want from me?' which can strike you when someone new turns their attention on you. It is as if a wave of suspicion is transferred from them. Perhaps this is justified, perhaps it is not. At least be open minded enough to try to find out.

Friendship is not a shackling contract. It does not immediately take you over and demand too much from you. There are few obligations which you do not want to fulfil. To be a friend does not mean that you are going to have to share your entire life with someone. A holiday friendship can be as enjoyable and life-enhancing as a friendship that goes on for years. If while it is going on, it gives pleasure to the people involved, it is a good friendship. Do not look for friends that must stay with you forever or who you think will greatly improve your life on a permanent basis. If your new friendship grows and endures over the years, that is good; if it dwindles after a time, don't worry. Never try to force it and above all, enjoy it while it lasts.

It is very important to make friends with people who do not look down on you. Try to establish yourself with people who regard you with some respect for no-one wants to be the tame lame dog, the 'friend' who is accepted as a cross and referred to as 'poor old so and so'. To avoid being placed in that category, don't spend your time moaning or putting yourself down. Have something of your self about which you are proud and make sure that it is not overlooked. Only if you esteem yourself, will other people esteem you too.

You learn to make friends easily if you have a good model to show you how. Gregariousness is a family trait, some people grow up in friendly households where the door is always open. Others are not so lucky. They have to learn the art of friendmaking in adulthood.

So how do you make friends? One of my friends, appropriately named Dawn, was brought up from babyhood in a family where all sorts of people were received in friendship. Today she has only to stand in a bus queue for people to start speaking to her. In crowded places strangers smile at Dawn, they make conversational approaches to her, in some way they sense that she radiates friendliness and that she will not criticize them. How does she do it?

In the first place she smiles a lot, her mouth turns up at the corners even when she is serious. If you want to make friends, smile first. A smile turns aside hostility and suspicion. A smile makes a stranger's face seem less threatening, less superior, less intimidating. Some of the people you smile at might raise an eyebrow in surprise or suspect your motives but that is their mistake, not yours. Far more people will respond in a positive way.

In the second place, as soon as a movement or a word is directed at Dawn, she speaks and she moves—perhaps only imperceptibly—towards the person who wants to talk to her. She does not freeze off a tentative approach but blossoms with interest. She makes the stranger feel interesting and important. Just by encouraging people to talk to her she has heard enough fascinating life stories to fill a library.

Dawn is a natural friend-maker but even people who are more reticent can learn how to open to others and expand their lives as a result. Knowing something of the technique of body language is a valuable asset. It seems a simplistic science to those who instinctively and unconsciously watch everyone around them but in fact there are some basic rules—take stock of how someone responds to an initial approach from you. Do they draw back, do they fold their arms across their chest? Do they sit back in their chair and cross their legs? If they do, they are on the defensive and if you are intent on winning them over, you will have to put yourself out to be as charming and as reassuring as possible. Lean—but not too far—towards them, look at their eyes which are indeed the mirrors of the soul. We can control every muscle of our faces but we cannot control our eyes. The pupils are the greatest give aways. Someone who is suspicious or hostile cannot prevent their pupils narrowing; as they relax and feel more confident, the pupils expand.

Living Alone—A Woman's Guide

## Making friends

Communicating with people you do not know is always difficult but the rule to remember is that if you smile at someone who looks interesting and they smile back but do not speak, it does not mean that they have no wish to talk to you. Both you and they are probably suffering from the same problem—neither of you knows what to say after you say 'hello'.

Someone has to break the ice and it might as well be you.

It is in fact a mistake to say 'hello' because all you are likely to receive in reply is another 'hello' back. Say something that needs thinking about, but not prolonged cogitation. Say something that carries a genuine attempt at communication.

The simplest way of starting a conversation is to say who you are and what you are doing in the place where you have met. This happened to me recently when a tall, white haired woman strode up to me at a gathering and announced, 'I'm Ruth Johnson and that's my husband Dick over there. We're from New York. . . .'

She gave me three facts at once, and no way could I, having been addressed with such directness, fail to reply with some information about myself.

Ruth turned out to be a very interesting and intelligent woman but her initial attack might make tender violets shrink. If you are less confident than she, or if the occasion does not merit a sort of identity parade, confine yourself to some gentler tack.

You can make a comment about the place you are in or the occasion. But be careful not to be too clever or too cutting. If you are at a wedding and allow yourself a catty comment about the bridesmaid, you may find that the person to whom you are speaking is the girl's mother.

As a rule avoid the weather for a conversational opener. That tends either to lead you into a thicket of platitudes like 'Let's hope for a better summer than last year' or 'Well, the garden does need some rain.'

If all you can think about however is the weather, break the conversational ice by telling your new acquaintance

26

how much you have longed for rain to water your begonias because you have entered for the local flower show. That's slightly more colourful and interesting than just a sigh and 'no rain yet, I see.'

To say something like 'turned out nice again' asks to be repaid with a straight 'yes' and then you're back where you started.

Try to avoid asking a question that could be answered with a direct negative or positive. Frame your question so that the stranger has to say something more in reply. If you can wheedle some personal observation out of the stranger, it is more easy to expand the breadth of the conversation from then on.

It is interesting to note the taboos about questions that should not be asked. For example the British shy away from any discussion of money and many of them dislike being questioned about their jobs. However as a journalist, asking questions and trying to find out about people is part of my work and I am frequently regarded askance in off duty hours because I forget that I'm not on an assignment and extend my questioning beyond the acceptable limits.

For several years I lived in India where it was amusing to observe the lack of inhibition Indians have about personal questions. It was very common for a complete stranger to ask; 'How much is your husband earning?' That question, asked in Britain, would throw a cocktail party into panic.

If the conversation does get off the ground, do not try to make yourself appear to be very clever or superior. Don't try to impress. Remember you are not entering for some sort of job interview, you only want to make friendly contact and to pass the time with another human being. You are not going to make a friend for life with everyone you speak to, so put all unreal speculations out of your mind.

On the other hand, don't make yourself out to be some sort of idiot either. The 'silly me' approach is sometimes used by women who are anything but silly and, to their chagrin, they can find people believing they are what they say they are. It is best to be true to yourself and never say something you do not believe or mean because only by telling the truth can you hope to establish yourself with the sort of friend you really want.

A conversational approach that never fails is to find some way of complimenting the person to whom you are speaking but take care not to make it look as if you are laying it on with a trowel, and again, take care that what you say is true. If a woman is wearing a dress you admire, tell her so; if a man has done or said something which you thought admirable or with which you agree, say so.

People like to be admired, they soften towards whoever pays them a compliment and if it is sincere, they are not likely to be hostile.

If someone says something nice to you, do not pass it off as if it is nothing. Too many people think it sounds conceited to admit to pleasure at being flattered. If something they have is admired, they immediately begin to underrate it, to talk it down—'It's just an old thing from the back of the wardrobe.' The correct way to reply to a compliment is to smile and say simply 'Thank you, that's very nice of you.'

In most cities today you can learn this sort of technique at a course in assertiveness training, often organized specifically for women. It seems to me that the title of these very admirable courses could be a deterrent to the sort of people that might benefit from them most, because 'assertiveness' is a word that has undertones of aggression and women are very afraid of being thought aggressive and too pushing.

An assertiveness course however can teach the pupil how to achieve greater poise in social situations and how not to be too easily put down. They learn through situation simulation to take pride in themselves and their own opinions and stand on their own feet.

For people who are in need of more intensive treatment than the courses, there are also Shyness Clinics in some places. Good doctors will be able to help patients find them.

One of the most interesting and cheering developments from the Women's Movement has been women's new awareness of and appreciation for friendship with their own sex.

To like other women and to enjoy their company, does

not mean that you will be suspected of having lesbian tendencies. Women today are now more appreciative of their female friends than they were a generation ago.

A young single mother told me; 'One of the good things about being on my own has been the support and friendship I received from other women. They have been my greatest support, I really appreciate them immensely. They fill a whole area in my life which no man could ever fill. Women's friendship is marvellous; I need the company of my own kind because I find they understand my problems and can give me more useful and impartial advice than men could ever do. When they are good friends, their friendship comes without strings attached.'

The best way of improving your confidence, of course, is to practise these techniques, whether you do it by chatting to strangers at the bus stop or if you take deliberate steps to increase your circle of friends or to find a lover.

Singles' clubs are often joked about but for thousands of people they have fulfilled their purpose of introducing lonely people to each other. Nearly everyone who joins a singles' club starts off feeling deep reservations but those are gradually overcome when they discover that the other people in the club are not all misfits of society but perfectly normal people who want to meet others of the opposite sex. Friendships as well as romances have been formed in those clubs and they provide a focus for many previously isolated social lives.

One widow said; 'I was really afraid to go on the first night but I relaxed when I realised that everyone there was in the same boat as me. You don't feel like the only person in the world without a partner when you go to a singles' club. You don't sit there all night thinking "What's wrong with me that I haven't got a man?" '

It is worth while looking for a club where you are likely to find the same sort of people as yourself. The biggest club is Nexus which has 10,000 members in most cities of the UK and the ages of the members range from 18 to 90. Nexus runs a comprehensive programme of social events where people meet in a relaxed and friendly atmosphere.

Other clubs which cater for people in specific jobs include

the Single Professional's Association which has six branches in the UK and 'vets' its members. There is also a central listing organisation for singles' clubs called the National Federation of Solo Clubs based in Birmingham which will supply details of clubs all over the country. Their address is in the appendix.

You find other clubs advertised in public libraries or at the Citizens' Advice Bureau.

If you are looking for a lover it is best to sort out in your own mind what you really require from your 'ideal companion' and then set out to find it. Age groups, income levels and social or family connections are not so important when looking for a lover as they are when looking for a spouse. A love affair is not as binding or as demanding as a marriage. If you do not intend to commit yourself entirely to this new person, don't pretend that you do. A casual relationship can be as satisfying and a great deal less fraught than one that is entered into with the hope of marriage. Lovers can more easily become friends when the understanding is mutual and the demands on each other kept as unconstricting as possible. Several elderly couples of my acquaintance have those sort of relationships. They would never openly admit to being lovers and they live in separate houses but they socialize together and take holidays together. Their problems of loneliness are solved without the loss of their independence.

There is always the option of the marriage bureaux, and they are still thriving, but they often find they have a glut of middle aged women on their books. However a recent addition to the 'bureau' scene is an organization called 'Old Friends' which was formed by a widow who recognized that middle age is often the time when the need for a companion of the opposite sex becomes pressing and more difficult to satisfy. All her clients are over 40 and they are not all looking for marriage by any means. Some want a companion for holidays or theatre outings while others ask to be introduced to people of similar interests and the same sex as themselves. A computer is used to match people up. The address of this organization too can be found in the appendix.

Those who are tentative about attending a club or exposing themselves openly through a bureau often use Personal Column advertisements in their search for a companion.

It is best to advertise in the kind of newspaper or magazine that you read yourself and also to be quite definite about the sort of person you are looking for. If you are looking for a man or a woman, say so, and give your own sex at the same time. Do not try to be too original or eye catching in your advertisement because that can cause trouble. One woman had a spate of letters with bizarre sexual suggestions after she innocently advertised herself as being 'warm and friendly'. Words like 'fun-loving' should also be avoided. Always use a box number and when you decide which of the replies to follow up, make a date to meet in a public place where it will be easy to get away should the need arise. Also never give your telephone number or address to someone, no matter how charming, who you meet for the first time.

One woman who advertised for a male friend said that the volume of letters she received in reply surprised her. 'They were all from nice, honest people who, like me were just lonely. I had no idea that so many men felt as isolated as I did and this has made me look at other people much more sympathetically now. I realize that I'm not the only person in the world who feels alone and unwanted.'

## Family relationships

Like friendship, the maintenance of good family relationships goes a long way towards helping people to live happily on their own.

As Dorothy Jerrome's Tremendous Ten knew, however, one of the problems with over-dependence on families is that unless they are closely monitored, they can take over and strangle what surrounds them.

'I've got my family, what else do I need?' is the sort of question asked by people who are in danger of stranding themselves in one way situations.

It is a mistake to place too much reliance on your family as your only support group. Children, forced into feeling responsible for the mental well-being and social integration of their mothers or fathers, inevitably resent the situation.

But just as you must never make too many demands on your family, never on the other hand, push them away if they do offer help and support. Only say 'I can manage, thank you' if you really can. Do not expect the offer to continue to be made if you brush it off out of pride or obstinacy. There is a place in the contented life for family as well as friends, the possession of one should never cut out the enjoyment and possession of the other.

Families extend as you grow older, nieces and nephews, cousins and second cousins, even god children, come onto the scene and it is good to be accepting and friendly to people of every generation. One of the greatest life enhancements that come to people as they grow older are grandchildren.

Today the image of the grandparent has changed for that stage often comes not in old age, but in middle age so the old fashioned idea of the helpless white haired granny or grandpapa huddled under a shawl in front of the fire, is totally unrealistic.

Successful grandparents are not pushed out of the family scene but are often more involved with their grandchildren than people were in the past and that has beneficial effects both for the old and the young. A child's link with its grandparents is extremely valuable, helping to build up its conceptions of the world and ways of behaving. The grandparent has the time and the inclination to pass on knowledge and appreciation to grandchildren, more time perhaps than busy parents who may both be working as well as bringing up a family.

Modern grandparents, perhaps because of increased fitness and mobility among older age groups today, are sharing more in the upbringing of their grandchildren, taking them for weekends or keeping them while parents are at work. Often too they find that not only do they have more time to spare but they are also in a better financial position to buy presents and provide entertainments for grandchildren than they had for their own children. To be a grandparent is like being given a second chance to appreciate the joy of a child.

Godchildren are often surrogate grandchildren for those who have none of their own and it is also possible to appreciate the company of the young by 'adopting' a grandchild. If there is a family in your vicinity that might appreciate the help of an adult for baby sitting or baby walking—offer your services. In some places there are local 'Adopt A Granny' schemes through which families without grandparents of their own ask an older women who lives alone without family to join them for outings or celebrations like birthdays and Christmases. This has proved to be a huge success in many cases.

If this idea is not attractive or feasible some people foster a child from an underdeveloped country. There are several organizations who arrange this and it means that the adoptive parent or grandparent writes to the child and receives letters back. The adoptee also contributes money towards the child's upkeep, often in an orphanage. Dr Graham's Kalimpong Homes in Northern India is a case in point and others like Action Aid are listed in the appendix.

From time to time people who adopt children far away go on holiday to meet their 'children' and many long standing and fruitful relationships have grown as a result.

# FOUR
# Strategies for Success

As well as taking positive steps to avoid becoming isolated and suffering from the problems of loneliness there are many practical things you can do to make the most of single living.

Strategies for successful single living range from having a pleasant place to live to keeping your mind and body occupied. Perhaps the most important area of life to organize first is what to do with your time.

'Get a job' used to be my standard advice to all widows who told me of their troubles. It seemed to me that I would have been moaning just as badly as any of them if I had not been forced into earning a living for myself after my husband died.

Going out to work has meant that my mind has always been fully occupied and loneliness kept in its own little corner. Of course it slips its lead from time to time but it has not been able to roam around at large for I have been far too busy.

If living alone is to be successful the mind must be occupied with either paid employment, absorbing hobbies or voluntary work. A job can be as undemanding or as engrossing as you choose to make it but take pride in it and try to do it well. Give it your full attention and it will develop into another part of your life.

However, it is a mistake, which I have committed myself, to allow your work to become so important in your life that it overrides everything else. You think about it all the time, identify yourself with it, mould your entire life round it.

Ask yourself if you are allowing your work to become a substitute for other things in life. This is dangerous because if you were to lose your job or retire, you would be in danger of feeling you had lost your entire identity and your reason for living.

34

Because of the claims of their careers, men are more in danger of making their work a surrogate for all other relationships than women but it is a hazard which all people on their own should guard against. Love your work by all means, take pleasure and pride in it, but do not allow it to fill your life to the detriment of your family, your friends, your hobbies and all other outside interests.

As work opportunities shrink and the numbers of redundancies loom ever larger, having a job has become more of a luxury, especially for those in middle age. To make up for the lack of a job, it is essential to keep the mind active and get out of the house into the company of others.

Voluntary work can impose a discipline and give an interest to people who have no paid employment or no financial need to work. Helping out at your local hospital, taking round Meals on Wheels, acting as local representative for a charity, manning a telephone for the Samaritans, being selected as a Marriage Guidance counsellor or working with children are all possible options.

It is worth remembering that your work may be particularly appreciated at times of celebrations, especially Christmas, when even the most self-reliant people on their own can feel twinges of loneliness. If Christmas looms bleak and lonely on your horizon, why not enrol with a charity that helps other people? In cities especially there is plenty of work available for helpers prepared to do some driving of old people or give up Christmas Day to serving turkey and plum pudding to pensioners or to homeless people in hostels. Put your name down with a local charity well in advance of Christmas so they know who they can rely on when the time comes.

It is also important to maintain other interests in life. 'It costs too much to have a hobby' or 'It's too much trouble to go out at night' are reasons people give for spending their leisure time slumped in front of the television set. However hobbies are essential to a balanced single life and they need not be cripplingly expensive.

Painting, for example is a popular hobby, although it is not cheap. However, if it is possible to stand the cost, there are opportunities for painting holidays, for classes and outings and for taking part in local amateur exhibitions if you really get keen and you don't have to be a Rembrandt to get immense pleasure from painting. The marvellous thing about it is that you are totally unaware of the passing of time and the release you get from your other concerns while concentrating on a picture is like going into a trance.

Evening classes, which are usually run during the winter, are within the budget of most people, especially since most of them offer reductions for pensioners and the unemployed.

There is a huge variety of evening classes on offer—from creative writing to the making of mediaeval musical instruments—but perhaps the most popular are practical classes like sport, cookery or dressmaking.

Sports, yoga classes and country dancing groups are good ways of keeping fit and increasing your social circle at the same time. If you want to make friends of both sexes, enrol in a class which will appeal to men as well as women—bridge, photography, woodworking or car maintenance for example. Classes like that also have the advantage of throwing you in with people of different age groups.

Many colleges and universities run extra mural classes which provide a vast amount of mental stimulation. There are also interesting summer schools held all over the country and a note about them is in the appendix.

Sometimes lonely people are tentative about signing up for hobby classes and if this is the case, start with a small class to which some of your friends already go. This will not present you with too many integration problems and you can move on to the bigger guns later when your social confidence is established.


### Holidays

All work and no play makes for a dull life and one way of adding spice and excitement to your existence is to take holidays. It need not be a trip round the world, for a day away to a different city or a weekend in the Highlands provides the change and the feeling of recharging the batteries that is the whole point of a holiday.

Saving for a trip away from home adds to the excitement

and keeping a 'holiday fund' provides an interest in the darkest and wettest days of winter.

A huge variety of holidays are available and are constantly advertised in every branch of the media. People travelling alone however usually tend to avoid the crowded beaches of the most popular resorts. These can be lonely places for anyone without a companion but if a sun holiday on the Costa Brava is what you crave, book with one of the groups that cater especially for unaccompanied people. Some of them specialize in holidays for people under 35 and others for the over 50s but there's one for everybody and they can be found by consulting any travel agent or reading the advertisements in Sunday newspapers. Some useful addresses are given in the Lifestyle appendix.

A more invigorating and active holiday is one that caters for specialist interests. There are bridge holidays, wild flower hunting holidays, hiking holidays and painting holidays in many different parts of the world. Again the small ads in newspapers help you find them as do specialist hobby magazines and radio or television programmes about tourism.

Taking a holiday that is an extension of your favourite hobby is a good way to make new friends with the same sort of interests as yourself and also increases your own knowledge of the subject.

*Single travellers*

One of the great complaints levelled against holiday companies by people who like doing things on their own is what is called the 'single person supplement'. This is an extra charge levied on those who want to have a room to themselves. Some companies and tours do not even provide single rooms at an extra charge, they just do not have any one person accommodation on offer.

This policy is called the 'Noah's Ark syndrome' because it implies that holiday makers, like animals in the ark, go two by two. For someone who appreciates living alone, to have to share a room with a stranger for the period of their holiday is a form of torture.

'I cannot abide even sharing with a friend for I need a

place where I know I can be alone and collect myself. It's essential for my well being and mental equilibrium. There has to be a period in every day when I can be totally alone', said one would-be holiday maker who had failed to find a trip that could give him the privacy he wanted. The result was that he did not take a holiday at all. The only way for holiday makers to change tourist companies' policies towards single travellers is to be vociferous in their complaints against both the single room supplement and the Noah's Ark syndrome wherever it is found.

Like living alone, there are distinct advantages to travelling alone. You can go at your own pace, see the things that interest only you without feeling selfish, deviate from a fixed route if you decide to do so, and, most of all, when you travel alone there is a greater pressure to make friends as you go along. Strangers too are less reticent about approaching someone on their own than they are about speaking to a couple or a group.

It is astonishing the warmth and friendliness that solitary travellers find even in the most out of the way places. Not everyone is out to fleece you or to do you harm. If you take reasonable precautions, dress simply and do not boast or throw your money around, you should be perfectly safe.

Arm yourself with a good guide book, a dictionary of the local language and a secure insurance policy in case you get ill or have your money stolen and take the high road with confidence. If you set out full of suspicion and distrust about 'foreigners', the people you meet will repay you with the same feelings.

## Pets

One of the best ways of driving loneliness out of your life if you live alone is to keep a pet.

There are six million pet dogs in Britain and the population is sharply divided in its attitude towards them. Some hate them, others prefer them to people.

The pet-loving proportion of society however is numerous, for 10 per cent of the population of Great Britain keep dogs and 9.6 per cent keep cats.

In recent years however there has been a strong anti-pet movement which makes young mothers especially anxious with scare stories about the illnesses which can be contracted from too close association with dogs and, less frequently, cats.

Public parks in many cities have become no-go areas for dogs because of the fear of infection being spread by dog faeces and it is true that canine mess in city streets and parks is both disgusting and unhealthy. Careful pet-owners, however, can teach their animals to mess in gutters or in specially selected places and there is a plastic scoop on sale, appropriately called a 'pooper scooper'. Caring dog owners go out armed with one so that they can clear away any traces of their less socially conscious animals. Dog hygiene can be enforced in public places so that in itself is no reason to ban them. What the anti-dog movement overlooks is the vast range of beneficial effects that cats and dogs bring to their owners.

There are many benefits to be had from keeping a pet. Dogs have to be walked; their day-to-day need for exercise ensures that the owner gets out into the open air to take exercise and to meet other dog walkers. In the park where I walk my dog, owners are recognized by their pets . . . 'That's Simon's lady. That's the man who walks Missy.' We exchange greetings, we get to know each other though we have never been formally introduced. Soon we are smiling and talking when we meet on the street or in the shops.

Another dog owner said that though she had lived in her city flat for several years, she knew little or nothing about the people she passed in the street every day. After she bought a dog, many of them began speaking to her. 'Now I recognize that my dog was really a sort of excuse for them, it gave them the opportunity to break the ice and talk to me.'

The life-enhancement given by pets has received official endorsement because medical authorities have discovered that people who keep a pet tend to be healthier than those who do not. The reasons for this can be varied and while one is likely to be the regime of exercise that pets impose on their owners, a more important one is the tranquillity and removal of stress that comes from the uncritical and undemanding companionship of an animal. Pets also provide an outlet for love and attention. Having another living creature on which to lavish love is very good for you when you live alone.

Patients with pets make better and quicker recoveries from illnesses for the rhythmic stroking of an animal's fur has a deeply therapeutic soothing effect which lowers blood pressure and slows down the heart rate to a marked degree. Keeping a cat can now be part of the prescription for a patient recovering from cardiac illness for example.

Until recently when my oldest dog died, for many years I kept two dogs and two cats and my life would have been much less happy and fulfilled without them. They slept on my bed at night and ruled my life. A survey of pet owners has found that I am not alone in my weakness towards my animals for 50 per cent of pet owners allow their pets to share their bedrooms and 35 per cent allow them to share their beds. Dr Bruce Fogle, a London vet who conducted the survey among his clientele, found a couple whose Great Dane commandeered their bed so they moved to the spare room.

Patch, my oldest dog, was extremely wise and was the recipient of all my private thoughts, fears, hopes and ambitions. Head cocked, she would sit listening while I expounded on ideas which had to be articulated in order to be fully perceived. She was a nondescript white mongrel but she had the kindest, most understanding eyes in the world. She was my companion through fifteen years of widowhood. I talked to her and she understood me, perhaps she recognized some words, who knows? When she died last month I truly mourned and in my garden there is a brilliant red azalea planted in her memory.

A practical advantage about keeping a dog that can be trained to bark at strangers, is that they bring security to their owners. Old people in particular feel safer in their homes at night if they have a dog for even a small, friendly one can sound threatening through a closed door and deter a would be nuisance or house breaker. During the five years my family and I lived in London all the houses in our row were broken into – some of them more than once. We were never burgled and a detective who arrived to investigate one of the burglaries said that because my dogs barked every time anyone came up our path, they were better than the expensive burglar alarms installed by our neighbours for warning off intruders. It did not matter that our dogs were actually eager to welcome visitors, the burglars did not know that and the dogs made a lot of noise.

Some people on their own are deterred from keeping a pet because they feel it would be too big a drain on their finances. However the costs are not prohibitive. A dog costs only its original purchase price, its food and its veterinary bills. It is not necessary to buy an expensive pedigreed dog because all over the country there are Dog Rescue charities and branches of the R.S.P.C.A. which will sell dogs or puppies for nominal sums. There is an extra advantage in this because you are giving a home and love to an animal that might otherwise be destroyed. The Battersea Dogs' Home in London always has a wide choice of pets available because every year they have regretfully to destroy over 9,000 animals for which they cannot find owners. Details and addresses are given in the Pets appendix.

As far as veterinary bills are concerned, if you live in a city there is usually a branch of the People's Dispensary for Sick Animals where pets are treated at low cost for pensioners or people on low incomes.

The average dog or cat only needs a once yearly injection against canine and feline illnesses to keep it fit (at a cost of around £10) and it is also advisable to have female animals spayed to prevent them being a nuisance at times of being on heat and avoiding a houseful of kittens or puppies.

Food costs are not high unless you decide to keep a voracious Alsatian. The medium sized dog costs around £1.60 a week in dog food which can be supplemented with scraps and bits of toasted bread. Don't forget to give dogs greens, especially scraps of parsley, in their food—it keeps their breath from smelling.

If space is the problem and if the place you live in is inconvenient for a dog, cats can usually be accommodated or, failing that try a budgie, a canary, a snake or a spider.

41

Some people keep hamsters—which smell, I find—or rats which are not to everyone's taste. But if you live alone, keep a pet even if it is only a canary or a goldfish. The bonus of happiness it will bring you is immense.

## Home life

The golden rule for living alone successfully is to overcome the puritanical fear that by making yourself comfortable you are being selfish.

It is essential to take every means of making life as pleasant as possible and there's no need to deny yourself anything just because you are not sharing the indulgence or benefit with someone else.

The reluctance to indulge oneself, even in the most minor things, is most often exhibited by women who find themselves on their own after having thought about their children and their husband first for years. The habit of self denial can continue because they find it impossible to shake off their sense of guilt at indulging themselves.

Forget those self denying impulses. Look after yourself when you live alone for a little hedonism can sweeten your life.

Take the trouble to cook delicacies for yourself, read the newspaper cookery columns and if a recipe sounds delicious, make it for yourself. Set the table, decorate it with a flower or a candle, prepare everything in advance, put out a napkin and all the right cutlery and sit down as if you were being served by an invisible butler.

If you are feeling low, cheer yourself up by buying a bunch of roses or a half bottle of champagne. Drink from your nicest glass and luxuriate in the experience of being wickedly self indulgent. My greatest self-indulgence is a hot bath with lashings of scented bath oil, the more exotic the better. I forget about how much it costs to heat the water and just lie soaking.

If you are going to live alone and like it you must try to make sure that the place you live in satisfies and pleases you.

Work out what it is you really want from life and choose your home accordingly. If bustle and people, access to theatres and cinemas are important, urban life is what you need. Others who prefer a more isolated life might opt for a country cottage and a garden. Do not be afraid to change from one situation to the other if your needs change. Because you started off in a flat, you need not stay in one forever.

Your home should express your personality. Pick furniture and fabrics that you really like, not what you think you should like. Buy a bunch of flowers even though no-one but yourself will enjoy them. They are not an unnecessary expense, the pleasure they give will be above money, especially in winter and early spring when the world outside seems bleak and hopeless. Every autumn, pot up a few bulbs of hyacinths and in the darkest days of winter they will grow and burst into flower like islands of hope in the middle of the sitting room.

Choose colours with care for the colour of rooms can subtly affect moods and frame of mind. If you feel you have outgrown a particular colour scheme, buy some pots of paint and change it for if you are switching from pale blue to soft pink you may well be expressing a step forward in your development. Always be aware of your own needs and listen to the promptings of your inner mind.

Select every item for your home with your own preference in mind because there is no-one else to please. It does not matter if what you like might be considered unfashionable. You are the one who has to live in the house; you are the only one who has the final say in what goes into it. Arrange the furniture so that you have your most comfortable chair in the most convenient place with the telephone close at hand and all the things you most enjoy around you.

I enjoy an open fire so much that the pleasure of seeing it leaping in the hearth outweighs the trouble of clearing ashes and carrying buckets of coal. A fire is a companion on winter nights and as I stare into its red depths my mind goes off on voyages of discovery.

The aim when you furnish your home is to make it so cheerful and welcoming that when you open the door after a hard day, your heart rises in pleasure at being home among your own things.

No matter how comfortable and content you are in your home, it is necessary to feel secure there as well, especially if you live alone. You have to take sensible steps to protect yourself.

It is important however not to lapse into a state of paranoia about the dangers that lurk in the world outside your front door. Don't allow those worries to cast a gloom over your life. The police in every part of the country run Home Protection schemes in which officers call and advise anyone who asks for their help about ways of making a home more secure.

Ways of making your home safe start with buying a stout front door. Especially in blocks of flats the front doors are often flimsy and would yield to a kick. Strong doors can be bought and fitted quite easily. Ask your local police for the name of a tradesman who will do this or consult the Yellow Pages.

Door locks should be the best you can afford and preferably have more than one. Leave a key with a neighbour who you trust. Flats with entry-phones are more secure than those with open communal doors; door chains and spy holes should also be used.

Don't ever open the door to anyone without first checking the chain is in position and finding out who the caller is. Never admit a stranger, no matter how polite and plausible, to your home. Always ask for warrant cards from callers who say they are from organizations like the electricity board, the DHSS or the telephone company. Never keep large sums of money in the house or let it be known that you might do so. It is a pity that people today have to be so suspicious of each other but it is only sensible to take precautions.

Keeping a dog, as has been already said, is a good way of protecting yourself and it is also a great help to install a telephone. Not only does it make it possible and easy to maintain links with friends but it is a lifeline in time of trouble. In cases of hardship and where a telephone is important to someone who is alone and housebound, the social services can sometimes arrange for one to be installed free of charge.

Be vigilant about your neighbours, be prepared to help and do not turn away thinking 'I don't want to be involved' if something out of the ordinary happens. The recent increase in local neighbourhood watch schemes, in which neighbours keep an eye open for suspicious happenings, has also helped to give an increased sense of security—and of belonging to an active community—to those who live alone. To build security round yourself make friendly contact with the people living around you. Speak to them, pass a cheerful comment when you meet for if you are open and prepared to help your neighbours, there will be someone who will help you if you are in trouble. Do not be too standoffish and independent. If you need help, ask for it. It is also a good idea to establish a routine with your neighbours and deviations from it will be noticed.

### Self-confidence boosters

The people who make the best adjustment to living alone retain a lively interest in clothes and in their appearance and they know that they can put on a good front to the world when they choose to do so.

If you know you look smart the knowledge gives you confidence. It influences both your physical and mental health so never 'let yourself go' completely just because there is no-one else who cares about how you look.

An interesting experiment was recently conducted with 35 middle-aged women living in California who had been treated by their doctors for depression. They all complained about feeling lonely and having no reason for living. The psychiatrist who undertook to treat them arranged for all the women to be given facials and new hairdos and they were provided with makeup kits which they were shown how to use.

Part of their recovery programme was to make up their faces every day and after a few months of this each of the patients reported that they felt much more optimistic and self confident and also that they noticed how strangers related to them in a less negative way. As a result of the confidence this gave them, they were more able to meet new people and the doctors found that they were also physically healthier.

Don't be afraid to be different, don't be afraid to be yourself. Forget about the strictures that have been placed on you for years, casting them off one by one if they seem irksome or unnecessary is a wonderful way of making life more pleasurable.

Try however to retain a sense of proportion, stay within the bounds of the law or reasonable propriety, for there is a huge difference between 'pleasing yourself', 'doing your own thing' and becoming a misfit or an oddity. People warm to a genuine 'eccentric' but they recoil from someone whose behaviour is disturbing or bizarre.

Practise feeling good about yourself. Gently tend your ego. Allow yourself a little selfishness and a certain amount of conceit. The inner core of every individual is like a tender plant that needs nurturing and unfortunately the old fashioned way of bringing up children in which parents told them to think of others before themselves and refrained from praising children in case it led to 'big headedness', meant that they grew into adults who were tentative about putting themselves first—or sometimes even second. Children treated in this way rely on others to reinforce their self value, to enhance their lives. They have no image of themselves except as part of a cohesive group, protected by family, lovers or friends from the outside world. Unfortunately those are the people who find it hard to cope with having to exist alone. But if they can sit down and look inside themselves with some admiration, add up their positive qualities and take realistic stock of their advantages, they will make a new assessment of themselves and this in turn will give them a new status with other people. The outside world is very prone to undervalue people who undervalue themselves.

### Peace of mind

If you have peace of mind, your physical health will benefit also.

There used to be a general assumption, among doctors as

well as among the general public, that those who lived alone were not only objects of pity but were at risk of suffering impaired health as well.

However, a doctor practising in Southampton conducted an in-depth survey of his patients and discovered that people who lived on their own had an overall chance of being fitter and living longer than those who were living with their families or in an institution.

People alone were more alert to their own physical state and so they tended to present themselves in the surgery in the earlier stages of illness where treatment could be more effective. Those who lived in company with others had their growing frailties covered up for them. The single people were more alert to the demands of their own bodies because they knew they had no-one to help them if their abilities failed.

They also pursued more outside interests and benefited both by companionship and also because their minds are kept active and alert. It is now proved that people who keep thinking and stay interested in things outside themselves for as long as possible are less likely to fall victim to senile dementia than those who slump into a state of mental torpor.

Dr David Weeks of the Royal Edinburgh Hospital said that he had several patients suffering from benign senescent forgetfulness who 'ought to know better' but they had given up on life and were making no effort to keep their brains stimulated. In America there is a research programme called the Philadelphia Project which is currently investigating how life and mental faculties are prolonged by continuing intellectual stimulus and creative thought. So don't stop thinking, don't stop learning, never stop reading the newspapers or trying your hand at the crossword puzzle.

The tranquillity that comes from well adjusted single living also contributes to overall well-being. People living alone are not subject to the state of undeclared war that many couples wage against each other, especially as they grow older.

Tranquillity can be introduced into life through relaxation.

Although you may think that lying back in an armchair and watching television is all the relaxing you need, this is not what is meant by deep relaxation. A regular regime of concentrated exercises can miraculously transform your life and your outlook. Writers and artists in particular find that ideas flow more freely and creative energy is re-fuelled by putting aside time each day for conscious and deliberate relaxation.

The way to do it is to sit quietly and concentrate one by one on the parts of the body. First tighten and then gently relax the muscles as you do so. Most people find that the head, the sides of the face and the tongue are most tense. When total relaxation is achieved a deep feeling of ease and warmth is felt.

Close the eyes and imagine that you are looking inwards at a spot in the middle of your forehead. It seems as if you are staring at a patch of soft black velvet. This appears to transform the brain waves into flowing patterns and a deep sense of peace fills you. In a relaxed state it is possible to control your blood pressure and to slow down your heart beat so anyone who feels even mildly under stress should learn how to relax.

There are many books and tapes on the market to help do it and once you have learned, do it every day. It doesn't take long but the benefits are incalculable.

One of the systems advocated by philosophical thinkers for bringing man into contact with himself is to practise a form of relaxation which involves sitting in a comfortable chair and deliberately cutting out all the swirling chains of thought that continually flow through our heads. Just look at the world outside and simply 'be'. By doing this you become an observer and the faculties of sound, smell and sight are enhanced. This exercise, practised a couple of times a day even while sitting in a train, at the office or at home, gives a deep sense of peace and adjustment which can transform your whole attitude to life.

My favourite way of inducing tranquillity is to stand in my garden.

Gardening is one of the most practised hobbies for it can be done by either sex and by people of any age. In fact it sometimes seems that all happy gardeners live to ripe old ages for gardening keeps you fit. Even when bending and weeding become difficult, you can replan your garden, make raised flower beds and grow things in large pots. If the garden becomes a little overgrown, look on it as a wildlife habitat, a paradise for butterflies and birds. The happy gardener welcomes a bed of nettles or a cluster of dandelions.

Keen gardeners attend lectures, go to garden openings or attend plant sales where it is possible to contact others who share the enthusiasm and because you have to garden in the open air, you see people in the gardens around or passing on the street; birds and small animals share the garden with you. Loneliness is quickly dispelled in a garden.

Having a religious belief and attending a place of worship both greatly contribute to tranquillity in the lives of people who live on their own.

If your local church, synagogue, mosque or temple is more than just a shell, it will have gathered round it a nucleus of people and organizations which in time will build a social framework and make friends for you. Doing the church flowers, joining in at sales of work or taking coffee in the crypt after services are all ways of making contact with other people and you also know that by helping with the work of the church you are giving as well as receiving.

However what is more important is the consolation and reassurance of true belief which can sustain and comfort you through all manner of trials and worries. As one woman said;

'I believe in the power of prayer. When I feel that my troubles are getting me down and there is no-one to whom I can turn for help, I pray. I lay down my burden in front of God and He never fails me.'

Appreciating what you have in life is a good way to find happiness in single living and a young woman who was widowed in her twenties after only a short marriage said that on days when sadness threatens to overwhelm her she literally counts her blessings. . . .

'I make a list of all the things that make me happy. It usually starts with the big things like health and my parents but pretty soon I get to the little things—like my new duvet and Marks and Spencer's Chicken Kiev. Sometimes the list is so funny that I end up laughing and it's a good way to banish the blues because you realize little luxuries are just as important as the greater concepts.'

# FIVE

# Managing Money

Money matters—it matters very much though high-minded people sometimes disdain to acknowledge its importance. It is often considered impolite even to mention money to friends but if you are to be realistic and develop to the full the potential of living on your own, a keen interest in 'filthy lucre' must be allowed to flourish.

The word 'money' should not be taken to mean a fortune. For most people their available money is a fixed sum which is very finite indeed. To live happily as Dickens pointed out in his character Mr Micawber, is to live within one's income, no matter how small that may be. For someone existing on only the state pension, an income of £10,000 a year would seem princely but the £10,000 a year man or woman will be just as unhappy if their outgoings are £10 more than their income. It is a matter of degree and what is important is that the money available is sufficient to supply the basic needs as seen by each individual.

'Living within one's income' has an ominously Victorian sound. It carries with it hints of cold houses and nourishing but unimaginative meals. That however need not be the case. Learning to live within your income can in fact be a challenge.

The mistake made by many people living on a small income is just to muddle through with their money, taking it in with one hand and spending it with the other.

The first thing that must be done if you and your income are to come to terms is to be clear headed about your finances and your outgoings. Sit down and make a list of your total income from all sources and on another page list your total expenditure. Remember to set aside a sum of money for emergencies because it is the unexpected bill, the overlooked liability, which can turn a well balanced account book into chaos.

When you analyse your financial life carefully in this way, areas of wastefulness and also possible ways of increasing an income can be more easily seen. Once the list has been made examine each entry with care. When studying income decide whether it is possible for it to be increased.

Are your savings in the most profitable places?

Could you receive a better yield somewhere else?

If you still need a little extra cash in hand, would it be possible for you to earn it or have you some asset lying disregarded which could perhaps be sold? The third use for a personal finance list is to scrutinize every item of expenditure. Looked at coldly there are sure to be areas where economies can be made. Even small savings can add up to considerable sums over the year.

If your financial problems are insoluble, it might be necessary to abandon pride and ask for help from some of the hundreds of charities that have money to disperse to deserving cases who fall within their scope of activity. Certain professions like acting or journalism have their own charities and so do ex-service associations or organizations like the Freemasons. If you want to find out if there is a charity that can help you, check with the Charity Commission at St Alban's House, 57–69 Haymarket, London SW1. They keep lists of all registered charities. If you find yourself getting into debt don't ignore the problem and hope it goes away. Speak to your Bank Manager or your local Citizens' Advice Bureau, and between you you will be able to look at the situation calmly and work out a solution.

Try self help first however. The devices people dream up for earning money are worthy of notice. A retired accountant found his local garage was only too happy for him to check their account books two or three times a week. They paid him partly in money and partly in work on his car. Payment in kind proved to be the most useful because it eliminated a large and unpredictable sum in his annual outgoings.

Baby sitters, especially mature baby sitters, are always much in demand and though their earnings may be small they find that a night's television viewing in a warm house with tea and biscuits provided means that they are saving energy costs at home. In a way too they are being paid in kind.

*Domestic economics*
It is interesting to note the devices some people use in order to economize. I used to write a column for a local newspaper in London and once asked readers for their money-saving tips. The letters flowed in by the bagful and they included hints of all kinds. One woman lit her fires with the waxed cartons used for milk or fruit juices—they are as good as firelighters and cost nothing. I know because I still do it.

Another woman who was a keen baker kept all the wrappers off butter to use for greasing the inside of her baking trays.

Keen walkers dragged home twigs to use as garden canes or firelighters; washing up liquid was diluted to half strength by several wily housewives who said it did the job just as well if it was half water.

People saved string and reused old envelopes; they hoarded laddered nylons for making polishing rags, stuffing knitted dolls or storing their onions from the garden over the winter (tie the onions one after the other inside the leg of the stocking and hang it from the roof of the garden shed). They even steamed unfranked stamps off letters.

One women aged 93 said that every spring she went out gathering the tips of young nettles which she brewed into a sort of cordial. Then she drank a glassful every morning as a tonic—cheaper and better than the stuff from the chemist's, she said. She believed that the nettle brew kept her alive and indeed her sprightliness was a magnificent advertisement for it. I tried it but it looked and tasted too horrible for me.

It seemed that everyone had a special way of saving money and they all insisted that their economies made an enormous difference to their expenses over the year, which I am sure they did.

*Reducing costs*
The expenditure list can also pinpoint areas where savings

can be made. Do a detailed analysis of each item of your outgoings and ask yourself 'Is there any way of cutting down on this?'

Could you reduce your fuel bills by insulating your home? There are grants available for roof insulation so check with your local authority about how much is available and which contractors they would recommend for the job. Roof insulation cuts a big slice off heating bills.

Double glazing is expensive and from recent research its effectiveness is not great enough to recoup quickly the cost of the work in fuel savings. What is almost as effective is old fashioned heavy curtaining for winter. Up until twenty years ago it was common practice for housewives to have winter curtains and summer curtains. The winter ones were thick and heavily lined but hung over windows and doors they acted as efficient suppressors of draughts. Good old-fashioned thick winter curtains can often be found in charity shops or in local auction sales. They will cut your heating bills for a fraction of the price of double glazing.

Electric blankets are deliciously warm at night but do not forget the old fashioned hot water bottle. A stone bottle wrapped in a bit of old blanket warms the bed no less effectively than the electric blanket and is much cheaper.

Remember too when you are adding up your fuel bills that White Meter electricity can work out cheaper providing you use the bulk of your appliances and heating overnight. During the day however the charges are actually higher than ordinary metered electricity, though this point is glossed over in the advertising brochures. So only go for the White Meter if you can strictly regulate your use of power.

The introduction of kitchen gadgetry means that people become used to using things which would have been considered unnecessary during the lifetime of their parents. Dishwashers, large deep freezes and electric clothes drying machines do make life much easier but they are heavy power users. When the day is fine why not put clothes out on a line to dry? What's wrong with washing the dishes in the sink now and again? After all, if you live alone, you need only put on the rubber gloves once a day for this chore.

Food economy is another way of saving money. The French housewife is famous as a skilled user-up of scraps. Nothing is wasted, leftovers are served up the following day in a new guise, scraps are popped into the ever-simmering stock pot.

Taken individually the savings to be made from imaginative use of left over food are small but added up over a year they make a surprising sum. Many people who live alone eat precooked or packaged meals and these are proportionately far more expensive than the same meals cooked from scratch at home. Cooking for one, as television cook Delia Smith has demonstrated, can not only be fun but can also save you money.

Even if you only have a small garden or can use part of someone else's garden or allotment, try growing your own vegetables. There is nothing more satisfying than eating food you have grown yourself—and you also know it is pollution and chemical free if you take care to garden organically (which is also much cheaper). For the price of a packet of seeds (around 30p)—and do buy the cheapest because they are just as good as the pricier ones—you can have enough lettuces or carrots to last you all summer.

Even flat dwellers grow herbs and vegetables in window boxes and on the market there are seeds for window box carrots, as round as little beetroots and very delicious. Once you become infected with the window box gardening fever, the possibilities are enormous. Everything from thyme and marjoram to tasty little yellow tomatoes can be grown in a window box.

Another hobby which can be used to cut bills is home wine or beer making. Beer kits can be bought in chain stores and chemist shops and wines made from the most humble and cheap ingredients like pea shells, elderflowers or rose hips can be delicious. Practice makes perfect and with care beetroot wine can be as tasty as claret—or almost. Home wine makers who lack the confidence to pass their brews off as table wines can use their wine for cooking and for making punches or wine cups when they entertain. There are many paperback books available giving recipes for wine making but remember that it is a lengthy operation and the longer you leave it to mature, the better it tastes. Wine left for a year at least can improve miraculously.

Wily food buyers take the trouble to shop around for the best bargains and they often patronize street markets. The time to turn up for the cheapest bargains is just before closing time—stall holders would rather sell their goods cheaply than cart them away to rot.

### Cut price wardrobes

My introduction to second hand clothes shops was in the early '70s when I wrote an article entitled 'Second Hand Rose' about the boom in shops selling cast off clothing. Since then the market has boomed and there is even a second hand clothes shop in trendy Covent Garden. It is possible in every town in Britain to find a shop selling second hand clothes for both sexes and all ages. Oxfam and War On Want are only two of the charities who have made money out of the public's enthusiasm for buying things other people throw out. Many people like me find it impossible to walk past a shop with second hand clothes and I have found some real treasures including an immaculate Burberry raincoat at less than a quarter of its shop price and a pale blue silk Chinese kimono embroidered all over with white waterlilies and herons which cost a mere £5.

A wily lady shopper who is very clothes conscious offsets her wardrobe expenses by selling clothes she is tired of to a used clothes shop or 'dress agency' and taking her money in kind. The best shops accept only high quality, clean and undamaged goods and they usually pay fair prices for anything of value. They are especially good places to look for an evening gown or for that special hat you need for a wedding. You can always sell it back again afterwards. Look for 'dress agencies' in the Yellow Pages.

### Profitable hobbies

People with special skills can always sell their expertise. Providing they do not earn more than the level determined by the DHSS authorities there is no danger of their state pensions being cut. A few extra pounds a week can make the difference between penny pinching and being able to treat yourself from time to time.

A woman whose family had grown up and left home kept up a lifetime of industry by knitting for friends and neighbours. In the beginning the gratified recipients of her jumpers and cardigans paid her with boxes of chocolates and fulsome compliments until she realized that her hobby could be turned into money. So she drew up a list of her prices—so much for a child's jersey, so much for an Aran sweater—and passed them around. She knits as much as ever because her charges are fairly modest but now she uses the money to pay for her annual holiday.

A retired hospital nurse whose hobby had always been painting turned it into cash when she started decorating anniversary plates to order for her friends. She bought plain white plates in jumble sales and painted them with details of babies' births, weddings, birthdays or retirements. Soon she had a full order book for her pretty plates which are treasured by the recipients.

Another money saving hobby is buying old furniture, china or books. This can become a time consuming passion. I started browsing round second hand furniture shops when I was newly married and had hardly any money. Modern furniture was beyond our pocket but that was not a matter of real regret because I learned to appreciate old fashioned furniture and my home is still furnished with the pieces I bought thirty years ago. Today however they have been aggrandized to the status of 'antiques' though many of them were regarded as 'junk' when I bought them.

Part of the fun of furnishing your home with other people's castoffs is the joy of looking for them. Nothing thrills the committed bargain hunter better than a really old fashioned junk shop with pieces piled one on top of the other and cobwebs hanging from the ceiling. It has been said that really crafty dealers keep their shops looking like this to make the customers think they are in a treasure trove. It works with me.

Visiting auctions too can develop into a full time interest. Going round house sales especially is the greatest fun in the world.

People are sometimes afraid of bidding for a lot they fancy or they fear that they will be 'driven up' in their price by the dealers. Don't worry about bidding, for even if you wag your hands around no-one is going to laugh at you. The thing to do is to position yourself near the lot you want to buy and make sure you catch the auctioneer's eye. As far as being forced to pay too much by the trade, always remember that no dealer will drive you up to more than he or she could sell the item for in a shop. Keep your head and you will usually manage to get the thing you have set your heart on.

Auction sale hopping not only introduces you to different, out of the way parts of the country but you meet new people as well.

Purchases in auction sales or junk shops can often turn out to be a secondary source of income for as your knowledge grows you will chance on something that you know is worth far more than its ticket price. Most amateur collectors end up doing a bit of buying and selling and they can make considerable sums. Ask your local auction house to put you on their mailing list and keep an eye open for sales announcements in your local newspaper.

Recently there was a letter in the 'Financial Times' from a man who had begun collecting old books while a student in the '50s. On the advice of a friend the books were sent to auction where they made the staggering price of £10,000, many times more than he had spent on them in the first place. The ex-student had not noticed the outlay of a pound here and a fiver there but when he received his cheque for £10,000 that was a very different story.

Another point to bear in mind is that the profits made on deals like that are tax free and there is also no Capital Gains Tax to pay. You do however have to pay tax on any interest you receive on your windfall when you invest it.

The aim of managing your money and keeping an eye on your expenses is to make life both more interesting and more secure. An author called William McFee once wrote, 'It is extraordinary how many emotional storms one may weather in safety if one is ballasted by ever so little gold'. With ever so little gold, you can live as you please.

# SIX

# Living on a Fixed Income

It is far easier to be happy on your own when you have sufficient money to make your life comfortable. Problems grow in importance and frustrations become overpowering when there is no money to help the sufferer either soften or eliminate them. Many women who live alone are on some kind of fixed income—retirement or widows' pension—so it is very important to make the most of every pound.

If you are retiring it is important which day of the week you choose to stop work. The newly retired, as opposed to existing pensioners, get their pensions paid on a Monday a week in advance so the best day to retire is Friday. If you retire on any other day you will miss out on a few days money that cannot be reclaimed. It is also important to make a claim for your pension in advance of the date of your birthday so it you have not been sent a DHSS form three months before your retiral date, write to your local social security office and ask for one.

If you are largely dependent on State benefits it is very important to be aware of everything that can be claimed. If you are in any doubt about what you are entitled to from state benefits either call at your DHSS office where there are leaflets to explain everything that is available or ask your nearest Citizens' Advice Bureau to help you. In November 1986 the level of benefits was altered by the Government and an up to date list of the basic benefits that apply to single people is given here:

Basic retirement pension          £38.70 per week.

Earnings limit for retirement       £75.00 per week.
pensioners
Women over 65 and men over 70 have
no earnings limit.

| | |
|---|---|
| Widow's pension | £38.70 per week. |
| Industrial death benefit which is payable if your husband or wife supported you and died through an accident at work | £39.25 per week. |
| Sickness benefit for up to 28 weeks off work if you are under state pension age | £29.45 per week. |
| If over state pension age | £37.05 per week. |
| Invalidity pension after 28 weeks off work | £38.70 per week. |

(plus another £8.15 a week if your illness began under the age of 60 for a man or 55 for a woman)

| | |
|---|---|
| Unemployment benefit for those under state benefit age | £30.80 per week. |
| For those over state benefit age | £38.70 per week. |

Supplementary benefit will be paid to bring your total income up to the following levels—for those under pension age and living alone, £29.80 a week at ordinary rate and £37.89 a week for long term rate.

Some benefits depend on your National Insurance contributions record so it is best to check with your local social security office to find out exactly what is due to you. Also find out if you can claim heating allowance or free prescriptions.

### Planning for retirement

To rely on the state pension scheme alone for maintenance in old age is a mistake since it now seems that by the end of the century the number of people taking out money will be disproportionate to the number paying in. As the government keeps pointing out, people should be making plans for their own pensions and there are various ways of doing this. The independence of living alone is made easier if you start early ensuring your own financial security.

The first essential for a long-term investment is security —will your money be safe? Will it be eroded by bad management or dishonesty? To say such things never happen is to stick your head in the sand. They do and they usually happen to schemes which sound like dreams come true. Avoid 'get rich quick' ideas if you want to be sure of collecting your savings again at the end.

*Pension schemes*
There are many independent pension schemes available and most of them are organized by large insurance companies. You pay in a fixed sum every month and at 60 or 65 you receive either a lump sum or a monthly pension for life which is related to the amount you have saved over the years. The earlier you start saving, the better pension you will have at the end because the more you pay the more you get back. Women who are widowed or who go back to work in the late forties or fifties would be well advised to 'top up' their pension schemes as soon as possible to provide a decent sum when they do retire. Most pension scheme funds spread their investments over a wide spectrum and so a fairly good appreciation on money can be expected but do not fall for the schemes that sound almost too good to be true. They rarely come up to expectations.

In the past two or three years people have become increasingly 'pension conscious' and there is a boom in the business as a glance at the financial pages of the quality newspapers shows. Premiums for a pension can be set against tax provided you are not already a member of a superannuation or pension scheme at your place of work.

The Inland Revenue permits an individual who is without a superannuation scheme, either by election or because they are self-employed, to contribute anything from 17.5 per cent to 20 per cent (depending on their date of birth) of their net earnings after deductions towards a personal pension scheme and the sum is then set against their tax assessment. The 17.5 per cent rate applies to those people under 50 and the percentage rises thereafter till people who were born in 1916 are eligible to contribute 20 per cent of their relevant earnings towards a pension and claim it against tax.

Of course the earlier you start paying into a pension plan, the better. If a self-employed person aged 30 pays only £25 a month into a scheme, they will end up with a considerable lump sum at the end.

The most common way of providing a nest egg for yourself is to pay in a fixed sum every month. If you cannot afford to pay your full entitlement in any one year, you are allowed to make it up the following year if your finances permit. When you sign the contract with the chosen insurance company you can stipulate that at 60 or 65 you will receive either a lump sum or a monthly pension for life according to how much you have saved over the years. In the event however, should you want to retire early, and providing you are over 60, most companies will permit you to take your pension or your lump sum as it stands at the time.

People who are in jobs that have an 'age limit' like airline pilots, professional footballers and ballet dancers can however purchase a pension which allows them to retire earlier. In the event of severe ill health which prevents you working, most pension schemes will allow you to cash in your policy.

*Pension policies*
There are two basic types of policy available. The first is the conventional 'with profit' method which adds bonuses to your investment each year so that in the end the sum you receive back is hopefully considerably more than you paid in. The second type of policy is more risky but potentially even more profitable because in using it you are investing your money in 'units' which have to be cashed in at the completion of the policy period. In effect you are gambling on the units increasing in value over the years. Remember however that it is a gamble and if your pension is all the money you have available it is often best to play safe. An advantage of the unit linked policies however is that they

are more flexible because you can take a few years off from paying in or you can switch your payments around more.

It is safest to have some money in both types of schemes and of course there is nothing to stop you having policies with more than one company providing your annual outgoings on pensions do not go over the limit set by the Inland Revenue.

It is most common for people who pay into pension funds to take their savings at the end in a lump sum and then look around for the best possible alternative investment available at the time of getting the money. Gains from life insurance policies are free of basic tax.

Remember it is extra important to make provision for retirement if you do not have the benefit of a company pension. Anyone who is in regular employment should check with their employer what sort of pension scheme operates for them—the majority of larger companies have one and if they do not, you should be looking for another job or making pension provision for yourself.

You can find the names and addresses of companies offering pension schemes by contacting the British Insurance Brokers' Association, at Biba House, 14 Bevis Marks, London EC4A 7NT who will send their list but make no recommendations for specific cases.

The best way to find which insurance and pension company suits your particular needs is either to approach the company directly or ask your accountant or an insurance broker for advice.

There are 'pension consultants' who will find out which scheme is the best for individual circumstances. Do your homework on your own as well however because some consultants tend to favour schemes which pay them commission.

Every individual's case is different and it is a mistake to accept the first option offered to you without researching the other offers or to succumb to a hard sell which some insurance companies inflict on those who approach them.

*Health insurance*
Another way of securing peace of mind if you live alone is to

know that you will not become destitute if you are ill and unable to work. Many insurance companies also offer schemes for insuring yourself against injury or illness and this is extra important for anyone who is self employed and is not covered by the State insurance scheme. It is however fairly expensive so it is worth while finding out about the various plans on offer from a selection of different companies.

Regrettably many insurance companies weight their premiums against women and levy heavier premiums on them than they do on men applying for permanent health insurance. The only way to stop this practice continuing is for women to protest as loudly and as frequently as possible.

It is also a good idea, if it is financially possible, to pay into a private health insurance scheme. Though the treatment you may receive as a private patient is unlikely to be better than that received by National Health patients, there is the benefit of being able to jump waiting lists which are sometimes years long in larger hospitals. In Edinburgh at the time of writing there is a 14 month waiting list for orthopaedic in-patient treatment under the National Health.

There are five main private health insurance companies operating in Britain and over five million people contribute to them either personally or through their employers' group schemes. These companies are listed in the appendix. They all issue brochures giving details of their various schemes available. If you are planning to enter such a scheme, the earlier you join the better. Rates for older people joining for the first time can be high.

## Savings

If you still have money to save after providing for your pension and insurances, use the surplus to add to your income. There are several ways you can do this.

*Bank Deposit*
First, and least adventurously, you can leave it in a bank deposit but you will receive a low rate of return, currently around 6.5 per cent. Some banks now however are offering

special high interest cheque accounts for depositors who are prepared to leave more than £2,500 in their accounts. Check with your own bank as the situation on rates is very fluid.

## Building Society investment

Secondly, you can put your spare money in a building society and receive a fairly high rate of return but no capital appreciation. You will never get rich—or lose the lot—if you use a building society. Each society offers different sorts of accounts and slightly differing rates so read the business pages of your newspaper and shop around. Every Saturday the Financial Times does an up-to-date survey of prevailing building society rates.

## National Savings

Thirdly, you can invest with the Government through National Savings of which there are several different types of investment accounts ranging from income bonds which give a return of 8.88 per cent after tax on a monthly basis for savers who are prepared to invest over £2,000, to a yearly plan in which you save sums ranging from £20 to £200 a month and receive a return of 8.19 per cent tax free.

In National Savings Ordinary accounts the rate is 6 per cent and the first £70 of interest is tax free providing more than £500 is left in the account. If you buy National Savings certificates you can invest up to £15,000 before you start paying tax on the interest. This is of especial interest to those who are in the upper tax bracket which begins to bite after annual earnings are over £15,400 per annum. National Savings are good for people wanting a regular income at a fairly high rate without risk and without capital appreciation. It is best not to put your entire capital into this form of investment but also to put some money into something which has a chance of increasing your capital. Suggestions for this are in the following pages of this chapter.

## Government stocks

A more profitable way of making your money work for you

is to buy British Government stocks which pay a bonus at the time of their completion after a stipulated period which can range from around 5 to 10 years. Some of them are also index-linked. They give a good rate of annual return ranging from 9.6 per cent to 8.3 per cent after deduction of basic rate tax.

### Premium Bonds

Premium bonds are for the optimistic investor because there is only one in 11,000 chances of winning a prize and then it is likely to be under £50. Out of 150,000 prizes disbursed by Ernie last year over 130,000 were for £50. Money left in Premium Bonds yields no interest, so over the years it is eroded by inflation.

### Stock Market mania

One of the most interesting and exciting ways of working with your spare money is to invest in the Stock Market. But remember this can be dangerous!

The Stock Market, pundits warn, should only be entered if you have money which you are prepared to lose, but of course there is also a possibility of increasing your nest egg quite considerably. Buying stocks and shares is like gambling and what you have to do is to survey the market and back your fancies.

You should not expect to win every time but there is certainly a better chance of making a good return out of stocks and shares than there is in betting on horses. In recent years there has been a great rise in the numbers of small investors who have been lured into the market by the launching of shares like TSB, British Gas and British Telecom—which made them money—and Britoil, which did not.

Stockbrokers have noticed in the past decade that more and more small investors, many of them women, are beginning to appear in their lists of private customers. Once bitten with the stocks and shares bug it is very difficult to shake it off, and women investors tend to back businesses which appeal to them for personal reasons. They buy Marks and Spencer shares, they buy shares like

Pineapple Dance Studio and Mothercare Habitat—and very often they make money.

The trouble with starting as an investor is that the Stock Market seems a very complex and intimidating area. But in fact having only a modest portfolio of shares can make you one of the company of investors and provide an added excitement to your life. The first part of a newspaper a keen market follower always reads is the Stock Market price list.

*Do your homework*
Before you start investing, read about the market and try to understand all the terms which crop up in market reports. Understand what a p/e ratio is and what is meant when a market is described as a bull or a bear market. There are many paperback books available explaining the terms used and the methods of working out the share market pages in the newspapers. Look for the simplest book you can find in the beginning and then progress to the more complicated ones. Your local library should be able to help and newspapers like the *Daily Telegraph* and the *Daily Mail* produce books which are cheap and very readable. There is a short explanation of the more basic terms in the appendix.

When you think you understand a little, start following the financial pages of your newspaper with a new enlightenment and only after that, start deciding which companies you would like to buy into. Do your own selecting and do not accept as gospel every tip you read in the newspapers. Some of my worst buys have been other people's tips. The ones I have followed slowly and selected for myself have been the best.

I am an unashamed Stock Market enthusiast and have had my disasters as well as my successes but the first share I bought nearly 20 years ago was Ladbroke's the bookmakers because I also come from a family of keen racegoers. It seemed a good idea to get into a business which had taken so much money off my family in the past. The share made me money and I was hooked. If I was to stop my minor forays into the market my life would be very much duller.

You do not have to invest thousands—a hundred shares

can give as much excitement as ten thousand and you soon learn when to sell and when to buy. It is usually advisable to take your profit and cut your losses early . . . 'leave a profit for the next man', is good advice. If you sell too soon and your share later reaches unprecedented heights, never repine. Having made a decision on the Stock Market it is a waste of time to look back in regret.

*Unit trusts*
A less risky way of investing is to buy unit trust shares. There are over 700 authorized unit trusts operating in Britain and eager for investors. To find your way around them it is a good idea to either buy or consult in your local library a book entitled *The Unit Trust Year Book* which is brought out annually by the *Financial Times*.

A unit trust is basically a fund in which small investors pool their money to buy shares and securities all over the world. The risk is spread because good unit trusts never put all their money into one company though most do specialize in special sectors or in selected countries. There are Far East trusts and American or Japanese trusts for example. The price of each unit varies, like Stock Market prices, every day and are quoted in the financial pages of the newspapers.

Money invested in big unit trusts is quite secure because they will be members of the Unit Trust Association which protects the interest of unit holders.

*Financial advice*
If you want to invest money and are in doubt how to go about it, ask your bank manager for help. Most managers are good at advising on worthwhile investments and all the big banks have special departments for helping their customers with investment problems. They will also buy stocks and shares or unit trusts for you. In recent months there has been a great upsurge in interest among stock-broking firms at reaching the small investor and 'share shops' have been opened in some department stores in larger cities—one of the first was Debenham's. Also most stockbrokers will accept business from private investors who contact them directly. Find your local firm in the

Yellow Pages. Remember you have to pay commission on each deal, so always ask what the charges are first.

No one likes paying income tax and though the basic state pension is at a level below the tax threshold, paying tax is an unavoidable necessity for most people. The old idea of the Tax Inspector as an enemy is out of date now and many people are surprised to find out that if they have any problems with tax, often the best person to help them out is their local tax inspector who will explain all the claims which can be made by each individual.

When you go to talk to your tax inspector, however, it is essential to put all your cards on the table. If you are moonlighting and pocketing the cash, it is best to stay away.

Remember that all redundancy payments under £25,000 are tax free and that there are tax allowances for people in the older age groups. If you want to read about tax matters the best book available is *The Which Book of Tax*, published by the Consumers' Association, PO Box 44, Hertford SG14 1LH.

People who are self-employed or have complicated tax returns with several sources of income might be well advised to employ an accountant but make sure before you start how much his or her fees are likely to be. Remember too that accountants' fees can be set against tax for the self-employed.

If you are fairly numerate however, it is however often just as effective and much more economical to do the job yourself—in cooperation perhaps with your tax inspector. There are many leaflets available from tax offices detailing, in much simpler language than was used in the past, almost every possible tax problem. If you want to retire abroad there are leaflets about that; if you are divorced or widowed, you can find a leaflet to explain your tax position. It is of course advisable to keep your tax liability to the minimum so always make sure that you are aware of all possible deductions.

*Making a will*
A word of warning! Even if you think there is no-one to benefit or inherit your assets after your death, it is

absolutely essential to make a will. It is possible to do this without consulting a solicitor and will forms can be bought in large stationers. Also *Which* magazine issues a guide on wills and probates which tells you how to make your own will efficiently. It costs £6.95 from The Consumers' Association, PO Box 44, Hertford SG14 1LH.

However because the law is liable to change from time to time and because lay people are not aware of the nuances of legal language, it is really a false economy to make your own will. Consult a solicitor and have it done properly. The cost will not be excessive and you have the comfort of knowing that your last will and testament is legal.

Above all, remember that the aim of managing your money is to make your life more interesting, secure and enjoyable. When you have control over your own money you can live as you like.

# SEVEN

# Buying a House

One of the best ways of securing a firm financial base for yourself is to buy your own home, and like investing in a pension, the sooner you start the better.

Over the past six years, partly because of the Government's right-to-buy policy for council tenants, there has been a rapid increase in private home ownership in Britain according to a survey by the Building Societies Association.

A recent survey showed that 77 per cent of people regard home ownership as their ideal and the proportion is even higher in the younger age groups. In all, 80 per cent of adults expect to be owner occupiers within the next ten years.

There have always been wiseacres who shake their heads and predict that the bottom is about to fall out of the property market but I have been hearing that story for thirty years and property is still a very good investment. I remember with regret a mews cottage in Chelsea which was on offer for £5,000 in 1959—an enormous sum then. We were persuaded not to buy it by one of the pessimists who said that disaster for property was just around the corner. To buy that mews cottage today I would have to produce a six figure sum.

## Mortgages

Most people who buy their own home do so on a mortgage. They have the double security of somewhere to live from which they have no fear of eviction providing they keep up the mortgage payments and, secondly, money which used to be expended on rent without a return can be used to buy a valuable and hopefully increasing asset.

Building societies look favourably on borrowers who are

already investors with them so the earlier the would-be owner-occupier starts saving, the better.

House owning is an extra advantage for a single woman because credit companies tend to regard property owners as better risks when issuing credit cards. Women who do not own their own homes are regarded with less favour than those who do.

There used also to be a prejudice against lending money to women but happily those days are now past and the societies realize that not only do many modern working women have as much money and purchasing power as men but they are also safer risks. Women tend to be more cautious with their money and default on payments much less frequently than men.

Some building societies are now offering pension linked mortgages which make good sense for people on their own. Again however they are more expensive than a repayment mortgage but if you have no pension provision or only an inadequate one, this would be a good way of saving. Always ask your building society to list all the possible options for you and do not allow yourself to be rushed into one.

*How much can you borrow?*
Before you commit yourself to house or flat purchase find out from a building society or a bank manager how much money they would be prepared to lend you. That gives a guideline for the price range you should be looking at. Remember that interest charges alone on every £1,000 borrowed can cost £8.80 a month if the rate for loans is 13.5 per cent as it has been on several occasions during the past few years. Banks' lending rates tend to be slightly higher than those of the building societies but often borrowers find banks more eager to advance money.

As a rough rule of thumb most people can borrow between two and a half to three times their annual salary or earnings before tax.

Most banks and building societies will lend around 85 per cent of the purchase price of a suitable property and there are even a few that will lend 100 per cent to people they consider to be good prospects.

Remember however that no matter how much you borrow, you will have to pay it back. This is usually spread out over 25 years but can be paid back in less time for people who come into a windfall though it is tax advantageous to continue paying it for the longer period.

At one time people in older age groups found it difficult to get a long-term mortgage but recently even those in their mid-fifties have been able to secure 25 year mortgages providing they are good financial prospects and the property they want to buy has a good resale value.

Once a mortgage is paid off, it is also possible for older single people to re-mortgage their house for an annuity and the loan is repaid out of their estate.

*Costs*

Estimate how much money will have to be spent on the property and whether after you have done everything you want to it, it will be capable of being sold for the total amount you have expended. Too many people fall for a dream cottage and get to work with schemes for improvement without estimating how much everything is going to cost. Never expect your first rough estimates to approximate to the final total. In matters of house improvement it is essential to be a pessimist.

It is also important to bear in mind hidden expenses. If you are trying to buy a flat, find out what expenses, roof repairs for example, have to be borne by all tenants and whether there are any standing charges for porterage or upkeep. These can often be unexpectedly high.

If there is anything that is complicated or which you find difficult to understand, consult a lawyer. It will be money well spent if it prevents you taking on a commitment that can turn out to be a burden. A final golden rule is never to sign anything until you have read and understood it. Remember too that the law pertaining to house purchase is different in Scotland. If you are buying in that country, employ a Scottish lawyer.

The property you have your eye on should be investigated thoroughly before you embark on any long term commitments. First of all make sure that the house or flat is suitable for you—not too big, not too small, not too far from your place of work so that you are involved in unexpected or unbudgeted-for travel expenses.

Make sure that it is structurally sound and not affected by any planning developments. Employ a local surveyor to check this out for you because he should be aware of what is going on in the locality. Also do some detective work on your own if possible because surveyors have been known to make mistakes.

Take account of whether the property is leasehold (which implies it is only yours for a fixed period of time) or freehold (which means it is yours in perpetuity). Check on the rating values of each property. Sometimes rates can be cripplingly high and they differ according to the locality.

# Summing Up

Some of the happiest and most confident people live alone. They look at life constructively and not negatively for they have learned to appreciate the positive aspects of their way of life.

The biggest bonus to be earned from living alone is freedom and self-determination. People who live alone enjoy the ability to develop their individual potential, make their own choices, guide their own lives. They know that their way of life brings with it an enhanced self-awareness and self-fulfilment that is often denied to people who share their lives with others.

Living alone should not be looked on as a penance or an aberration. It is a way of life adopted by choice and that choice brings with it the possibility of infinite variety. People who make a success of living alone know that, like everything else worth having in life, it has to be worked at but the end result is very worth while. As Winston Churchill wrote: 'Solitary trees, if they grow at all, grow strong.'

# Appendices and
# Useful Addresses

# Lifestyle

*ACTION AID*, Hamlyn House, Archway, London N19 5PS, 01-281-4101. For sponsoring a child overseas.

*ASSOCIATION FOR PROMOTING RETREATS*, Liddon House, 24 South Audley Street, London W1Y 5DL, 01-493-3534. Publishes an annual magazine called 'Vision' with a list of places where people of all denominations, and even non Christian, can go on retreat. Locations range from Bec in Normandy, or Iona to Eire.

*BIRMINGHAM SETTLEMENT*, 318 Summer Lane, Birmingham B19 3RL, 021-359-3562. Works to relieve loneliness and isolation by anticipating problems as well as helping to solve them. Has a Money Advice Centre, a gymnasium and Bodycare centre and a Mid Life Centre which is particularly good for the problems of people in middle life.

*BRITISH ASSOCIATION FOR LOCAL HISTORY*, The Mill Manager's House, Cromford Mill, Mill Road, Matlock, Derbyshire DE4 3RQ, 062-982-3768. Tells how to go about researching the history of your district.

*BRITISH INSURANCE BROKERS' ASSOCIATION*, Biba House, 14 Bevis Marks, London EC4A 7NT. Provides lists of insurance broking and pension companies that are among their members but makes no recommendations.

*CIPFA SERVICES*, 232 Vauxhall Bridge Road, London SW1, 01-638-6361. For list of Local Authority Bonds.

*CRISIS AT CHRISTMAS*, 212 Whitechapel Road, London E1, 01-377-0489. Organization that works in the field of homelessness and runs an annual Open Christmas for the homeless in London. Always needs extra voluntary helpers.

CROSSROADS CARE ATTENDANT SCHEME TRUST, 281 Liverpool Road, London N1, 01-607-6963. Provides 'sitters' to look after elderly relatives to give carers a break. Contact this address or Social Services for local groups.

DR GRAHAM'S HOMES, Room 216, South Bank House, Black Prince Road, London SE1 7SJ, 01-735-8171 ext 66. Sponsorship of children in Kalimpong, North India. The Homes have almost 600 boarders and between 200 and 300 day scholars. The primary care is for needy Anglo Indian children mostly from the slums of Calcutta with some from refugee camps in the northern borders.

ECOLOGY BUILDING SOCIETY, 43 Main Street, Cross Hills, West Yorks BD20 8TT, 0535-35933. Lends money for projects that help the environment like sound but derelict inner city houses and organic smallholdings.

ETHICAL INVESTMENT RESEARCH AND INFORMATION SERVICE, 9 Poland Street, London W1V 3DG (don't phone) sells information on stock companies telling where and how they operate. £35 for details of 20 FT Index quoted companies.

FAWCETT SOCIETY, 46 Harleyford Road, London SE11 5AY, 01-587-1287. Campaigners for equality between the sexes since 1866. Campaigns for tax equality and for more women in Parliament and local government etc. The Fawcett Society Library in the City of London Polytechnic is Britain's largest collection of literature and historical data relating to the women's movement since 1572. Welcomes active and supportive members of both sexes.

GREATER LONDON ASSOCIATION FOR PRE-RETIREMENT, 19 Old Jewry, London EC2 8EY, 01-601-4484.

LEISURE SERVICES FOR DISADVANTAGED PEOPLE, 36 Old Queen Street, London SW1. No phone.

MERCURY PROVIDENT SOCIETY, Orlington House, Lewes Road, Forest Row, Sussex. RH18 5AA, 0342-823922. A friendly society that lends for things like alternative treatment centres etc.

*NATIONAL ASSOCIATION OF CITIZENS' ADVICE BUREAUX*, 110 Drury Lane, London WC2B 5SW, 01–833–2181. *SCOTTISH ASSOCIATION OF CITIZENS' ADVICE BUREAUX*, 82 Nicolson Street, Edinburgh, 031–667–0156. See also telephone book for local and provincial branches.

*NATIONAL COUNCIL FOR CARERS AND THEIR ELDERLY DEPENDANTS*, 29 Chilworth Mews, London WC2 3RG, 01–2621–451/2.

*NATIONAL COUNCIL OF WOMEN OF GREAT BRITAIN*, 34 Lower Sloane Street, London SW1W 8BP, 01–730–0619. Aims at improving the quality of life for women and acts as a pressure group. Special committees for topics like health, housing, mass media, status and employment of women etc. Network of regions and branches in UK and also 74 countries abroad have similar National Councils of Women. International Conferences.

*NATIONAL HOUSEWIVES' REGISTER*, 245 Warwick Road, Solihull, West Midlands B92 7AH, 021–706–1101. For women of enquiring minds to meet each other for discussions.

*PRE-RETIREMENT ASSOCIATION*, 19 Undine Street, Tooting, SW17, 01–767–3225/6.

*REACH (Retired Executives Action Clearing House)* 89 Southwark Street, London SE1 0HD, 01–928–0452. Helps retired executives to work on an expenses only basis for charities and voluntary organizations.

*REDRESS*, 51 Endell Street, Covent Garden, London. No phone listed. Good quality second hand clothes shop.

*SAM-YE-LING TIBETAN CENTRE*, Eskdalemuir, Langholm, Dumfriesshire, 05416–232. The 'Buddhist Oxford' and a retreat for non-Buddhists as well as Buddhists.

*SAVE THE CHILDREN FUND*, Mary Datchelor House, 17 Grove Lane, Camberwell, London SE5 8RD, 01–703–5400. Britain's largest international children's charity concerned with the rescue in disaster and the longer term welfare of children irrespective of country, nationality, race or religion.

Always needs volunteers to help and also gifts. Sister organizations;

*Australian Save the Children Fund*, PO Box 486, Fyshwick, A.C.T., Australia 2609;

*New Zealand Save the Children Fund*, PO Box 9235, Christchurch 2, New Zealand;

*Canadian Save the Children Fund*, 720 Spadina Avenue, Suite 400, Toronto, Ontario M5S 2W3, Canada;

*Save the Children USA*, Amsave, 54 Wilton Road, Westport, Connecticut 06881, USA;

*Red Barnet (Denmark)*, 4 Brogaardsvaenget, DK 2820 Gentofte, Denmark;

*Redd Barna (Norway)*, Jernehanetorget 2, 0105 Oslo, Norway.

# Advice on Health

*ACCEPT*, Western Hospital, 200 Seagrave Road, London SW6, 01-381-3155 and The Broadway Clinic, Broadway, Wealdstone, Harrow, 01-427-3155. National network of counselling and treatment for problem drinkers and tranquillizer misusers. Also runs a Jobfinders and New Careers programme. Good publications.

*ACTION ON PHOBIAS*, 8-9 The Avenue, Eastbourne, Sussex. No phone listed. Helps create community based self help groups for phobics, especially agoraphobics.

*AGE CONCERN'S INSTITUTE OF GERONTOLOGY*, in conjunction with King's College Hospital, London, for improving the well being of the aged, Bernard Sunley House, 60 Pitcairn Road, Mitcham, Surrey CR4 2LL, 01-640-5431.

*ALCOHOL CONCERN*, 305 Gray's Inn Road, London WC1, 01-833-3471. A national charity to raise public awareness of the problems alcohol can cause, to improve services for people who drink too much and to promote preventive action at a local and national level. Runs information centres to provide counselling, information and advice. Associated with:
  *Centre National de Defense contre l'Alcoolisme*, 20 Rue Saint Fiacre, 75002 Paris;
  *Schweizerische Fachstelle fur Alkoholprobleme*, Postfach 1063, 1001 Lausanne, Switzerland;
  *Deutsche Haupstelle Gegen die Suchtgefahren E.V.*, Postfach 109, Westring 2, 4700 Hamm 1, West Germany;
  *ALAC (Alcohol Liquor Advisory Council)*, Aurora House, 62 The Terrace, Wellington 1, New Zealand;
  *National Council on Alcoholism*, 12 W.21 Street, New York, NY 10010, USA.

*ALCOHOLICS ANONYMOUS*, 11 Redcliffe Gardens, London SW10, 01-352-9779. For local branches, see telephone book. Branches in 110 different countries from Australia to Zambia and Zimbabwe.

*BRITISH HOLISTIC MEDICAL ASSOCIATION*, 179 Gloucester Place, London NQW1 6DX, 01-262-5299. Relaxation classes and tapes by post.

*BROOK ADVISORY CENTRE*, 233 Tottenham Court Road, London W1P 9AE, 01-580-2992/323-1522. Psycho-sexual counselling.

*CLINIC FOR CANCER PREVENTIVE ADVICE*, 6 New Road, Brighton, East Sussex, 0273-727213. Sends out free brochures and sells booklets with details of healthy living and how to avoid cancer, high blood pressure, coronary trouble etc.

*CORONARY PREVENTION GROUP*, 60 Great Ormond Street, London WC1N 3HR, 01-833-3687. Provides information on the cause of heart attacks and advises on action to reduce the risks. Very good leaflets. Related to the following organizations overseas:

*The National Heart Foundation of Australia*, PO Box 2, Woden ACT 2606, Australia;

*The American Heart Association*, 44 East 23rd Street, New York, NY 10010, USA;

*The National Heart Foundation of New Zealand*, Dept of Cardiology, the Princess Margaret Hospital, Cashmere Road, Christchurch 2, New Zealand;

*The Canadian Heart Foundation*, Suite 1200, One Nicholas Street, Ottawa, Ontario, Canada K1N 7B7;

*The All India Heart Foundation*, 4874 Ansari Road, 24 Darya Ganj, New Delhi, 10002, India;

*The Danish Heart Foundation*, Hauser Plads 10, 1127 Copenhagen, Denmark;

*The Finnish Heart Foundation*, Frederikink 20B, 00120 Helsinki 12, Finland;

*Hopital Tenon*, 4 Rue de la Chine, 75970 Paris Cedex, France;

*WHO Collaborating Unit for Research and Training in Cardio-*

*vascular Disease*, Ruprecht-Karls-Universitat Abteilung Klinische Sozialmedizin, Bergheimer Strasse 58, 6900 Heidelberg 1, Germany;

*The Netherlands Heart Foundation*, The Hague, Sophialaan 10, Netherlands;

*International Society and Federation of Cardiology*, PO Box 117, CH 1211 Geneve 12, Switzerland;

*Fundacion Hispana de Cardiologia Murcia*, 11 Entreplanta, 28045 Madrid, Spain.

*DR DAVID WEEKS*, Royal Edinburgh Hospital, Morningside, Edinburgh, 031-447-2011. Loneliness survey.

*HEALTH EDUCATION COUNCIL*, 78 New Oxford Street, London W1, 01-631-0930. Alcohol information packs, general information about healthy living.

*HEART TO HEART*, Mrs Joan Richardson OBE, PO Box No 7, High Street, Pershore, Worcs. Please don't try to phone, just write. Mrs Richardson has set up a network of people who have undergone heart surgery and who are prepared to counsel and advise others about to have similar operations.

*INSTITUTE OF BEHAVIOUR THERAPY*, 25 Abingdon Road, London W8, 01-938-1011. Cassettes on anxiety management.

*KEEP FIT ASSOCIATION*, 16 Upper Woburn Place, London WC1H 0QG, 01-387-4349. Helps women of all ages and aptitudes to make full use of their physical and intellectual capacities.

*MIND*, National Association for Mental Health, 22 Harley Street, London W1, 01-637-0741. Part of the World Federation for Mental Health which promotes the rights and interests of people with mental illness and also good practice in mental care. Produces factsheets on themes like depression, phobias and counselling in bereavement.

*POSITIVE HEALTH CENTRE*, 101 Harley Street, London W1, 01-935-1811. Training in relaxation and meditation. Programme of meditation free of charge two evenings a week.

*RELAXATION FOR LIVING*, Dunesk, 29 Burwood Park Road, Walton on Thames, Surrey, 0932-27826. Tapes and literature about meditation and relaxation.

*TURNING POINT*, 3rd Floor, Cap House, 9-12 Long Lane, London EC14 9HA, 01-606-3947. Operates 30 projects in England and one in Scotland providing information, advice and counselling for those suffering from alcohol or other drug related problems. For details of similar agencies abroad contact Mr Arthur Tongue, International Council of Alcohol and Addictions, Case Postale 140, 1001 Lausanne, Switzerland.

*WOMEN'S NATIONAL CANCER CONTROL CAMPAIGN*, 1 South Audley Street, London W1Y 5DQ, 01-499-7532. Hamlyn House, Archway, London N19 5PS.

*Private medical insurance plans*

*BRISTOL CONTRIBUTORY WELFARE ASSOCIATION*, Bristol House, 40-56 Victoria Street, Bristol BS1 6AB, 0272-293742.

*BRITISH UNITED PROVIDENT ASSOCIATION (BUPA)*, Provident House, Essex Street, London WC2, 01-353-9451.

*CRUSADER INSURANCE PLC*, Health Care Dept,. Reigate, Surrey RH2 8BS, 07372-42424.

*PRIVATE PATIENTS' PLAN (PPP)*, Tavistock House South, Tavistock Square, London WC1, 01-388-2468.

*WESTERN PROVIDENT ASSOCIATION*, Freepost, Bristol BS1 5YT, 0272-273241.

*Private Hospitals*

*CHURCHILL CLINIC*, 80 Lambeth Road, London SE1, 01-928-5633.

*CROMWELL HOSPITAL*, Cromwell Road, London SW5, 01-370-4233.

*DEVONSHIRE HOSPITAL*, 29 Devonshire Street, London W1, 01-486-7131.

*FITZROY NUFFIELD HOSPITAL*, 10 Bryanston Place, London W1, 01-723-1288.

*HUMANA HOSPITAL WELLINGTON*, Wellington Place, London NW8, 01-586-5959.

*LISTER HOSPITAL*, Chelsea Bridge Road, London SW1, 01-730-3417.

*LONDON CLINIC*, 20 Devonshire Place, London W1, 01-935-4444.

*PRINCESS GRACE HOSPITAL*, 42 Nottingham Place, London W1, 01-486-1234.

*NIGHTINGALE BUPA HOSPITAL*, 19 Lisson Grove, London NW1, 01-723-1288.

Further lists of private hospitals are provided by individual insurance companies.

# Social Clubs and Organizations

A selection of some of the many social clubs that operate throughout the UK. For a fuller London selection consult the pages of *Time Out*.

*BREAKAWAY*, 57 Garrick Close, London W5 1AT, 01-991-2169. A social club for single professionals aged between 23 and 43 with over 3,000 members in London and the Home Counties. Holds over 200 different events at separate venues each month.

*CONTACT*, 15 Henrietta Street, Covent Garden, London WC2 8QH, 01-240-0630. Encourages people living alone to develop their social interests by bringing companionship into their lives and to encourage helpers to give their spare time to these purposes.

*DATELINE*, Dept OAE, 23-25 Abingdon Road, London W8, 01-938-1011. Computer dating club.

*HI-SOCIETY*, Anthony Harrison, 01-586-5789. Social club that raises money for charity through its events.

*LONDON VILLAGE*, 01-586-7455. For 'friendly, presentable people' aged between 20 and 45. Likes to interview possible members and for this reason holds introductory evenings every Friday at the Charing Cross Hotel in the Strand. Over 3,000 members and large social programme for Greater London residents.

*INTERVARSITY CLUB*, 3-5 The Piazza, Covent Garden WC2E 8HF, 01-240-2525. Social club for graduates.

*KALEIDOSCOPE*, 57 Garrick Close, London W5 1AT, 01-997-8684. On the same lines as Breakaway but for people aged 37 and upwards.

*OUTSIDERS CLUB*, Tuppy Owens, Box 4ZB, London W1A

4ZB, 01-741-3332. A contact club and marriage bureau with an international network run by the Social Habilitation and Integration Trust for Disabled People. Good for those who feel lonely or emotionally stranded. Opportunities for people to meet and classes in conversation, social skills and relationship development. Most, but not all, the social events are in London but people come from all over the country and abroad to the club. Good library with books sent by post. Only other club with similar objectives is in Los Angeles.

*NATIONAL ASSOCIATION OF WOMEN'S CLUBS*, 5 Vernon Rise, King's Cross, London WC1X 9CP, 01-837-1434. Run on the same lines as the Townswomen's Guilds and has over 600 non political and non sectarian clubs which hold weekly meetings for women throughout the UK. Also organizes conferences and weekend schools. Provides lists of speakers for the clubs. Some clubs arrange holiday groups in Great Britain and the UK.

*NATIONAL FEDERATION OF SOLO CLUBS*, Ruskin Chambers, 191 Corporation Street, Birmingham B4 6RP, 021-236-2879. Social club founded 21 years ago by a widow, Mrs Paula Slater Greaves, for separated, divorced and widowed people aged between 21 and 65 who were suffering from loneliness. Sends out lists of all the venues throughout the UK where the clubs are held.

*NEXUS*, Blackstock Road, London N4, 01-359-7656. Largest organization for meeting friends of both sexes. Also active in Australia.

*OLD FRIENDS*, 18A Highbury New Park, Highbury, London N5 2DB, 01-226-5432. For people over 40. Introductions arranged by computer matching. Some overseas members who are anxious to make friends in the UK.

*SINGLE PROFESSIONALS ASSOCIATION*, (write only) c/o Family Centre, Good Housekeeping, 72 Broadwick Street, London W1V 2BP.

# Pets

*ANIMAL WELFARE TRUST*, Miss Patricia Fraser, Tyler's Way, Watford Bypass, Watford, Herts WD2 8HQ, 01–950–8215/0177. Finds homes for unwanted cats and dogs and runs 'Pet Concern' which assists with boarding fees for the pets of senior citizens in hospital.

*BATTERSEA DOGS' HOME*, 4 Battersea Park Road, London SW8, 01–622–3626. For finding a dog that needs a home.

*CATS PROTECTION LEAGUE*, 17 King's Road, Horsham, West Sussex RH13 5PP, no tel. Rescues and rehouses stray cats.

*NATIONAL CANINE DEFENCE LEAGUE*, 1 and 2 Pratt Mews, London NW1 0AD, 01–388–0137. Rescues and finds new homes for stray dogs.

*P.D.S.A. (People's Dispensary for Sick Animals)*, P.D.S.A. House, South Street, Dorking, Surry RH4 2LB, 0306–888291. A charity dependent on public support that runs 57 animal treatment centres and 36 auxiliary centres in the U.K. Pet owners dependent on State Benefits have their animals treated free of charge. Large range of leaflets about keeping various pets. Nationwide in UK and branches also in Cairo, Tangier, Cape Town, Soweto and Johannesburg.

*PRO-DOGS NATIONAL CHARITY*, National Head Office, Rocky Bank, New Road, Ditton, Kent ME20 6AD, 0732–848499. Started in 1976 by Mrs Lesley Scott Ordish to combat growing intolerance to dogs. Its slogan is 'dogs deserve better people'.

*PRO-ACTIVE DOGS THERAPY*, same address and telephone number. Started in 1983. Over 2,000 members who take their pets to give 'tailwagging psychotherapy' to old people in hospitals and residential homes.

*R.S.P.C.A. (Royal Society for the Prevention of Cruelty to Animals),*
The Causeway, Horsham, Sussex RH12 1HG, 0403-64181.
Inspector service, animal hospitals, clinics, subsidies for
veterinary fees for the pets of elderly people etc. Encourages
and assists similar societies all over the world.

# Help with Financial Problems

*AGE CONCERN*, Bernard Sunley House, 60 Pitcairn Road, Mitcham, Surrey CR4 2LL, 01-640-5431.
   *AGE CONCERN SCOTLAND*, 33 Castle Street, Edinburgh, 031-225-5000;
   *AGE CONCERN WALES*, 1 Park Grove, Cardiff, 0222-371-566;
   *AGE CONCERN NORTHERN IRELAND*, 128 Great Victoria Street, Belfast 2, 0232-45729.
   Wide range of services from day care to specialist services for physically and mentally frail old people. Campaigns and publishes a wide range of handbooks for older people. Branches of Age Concern in Jamaica and New Zealand and it is also associated with *EUROLINK AGE* which represents the interests of older citizens to the official institutions of the European Community. Eurolink Age can be contacted at Bernard Sunley House.

*ARMY BENEVOLENT FUND*, Duke of Yorks HQ, Chelsea Barracks, London SW3, 01-730-5388. Charity that helps ex-army personnel and their dependants.

*ASSOCIATION OF CHARITY OFFICERS*, c/o RICS Benevolent Fund, 2nd Floor, Tavistock House North, Tavistock Square, London WC1H 9RJ, 01-387-0578. For advice on benefits and addresses of helpful organizations.

*ROYAL BRITISH LEGION*, 49 Pall Mall, London SW1, 01-930-8131. Also *ROYAL BRITISH LEGION SCOTLAND*, New Haig House, Logie Green Road, Edinburgh, 031-557-2782. Helps ex service people and their dependants.

*CHARITY COMMISSION*, St Albans House, 57-69 Haymarket, London SW1, 01-214-6000. For information on all registered charities.

*CIVIL SERVICE BENEVOLENT FUND*, Watermead House, Sutton Court Road, Sutton, Surrey, 01–642–8511. Helps ex-civil servants.

*COUNCIL FOR SOCIAL SERVICES*, 94 Tweedy Road, Bromley, Kent, 01–464–2287/8.
  *SCOTTISH COUNCIL FOR SOCIAL SERVICES*, 18/19 Claremont Crescent, Edinburgh, 031–556–3882. Information on charities, trust funds and solo clubs.

*DISTRESSED GENTLEFOLKS AID ASSOCIATION*, Vicarage Gate House, Vicarage Gate, Kensington, London W8 4AQ, 01–229–9341/6. Allowances or grants for professionals in need or distress.

*NATIONAL ASSOCIATION OF CITIZENS' ADVICE BUREAUX*, 110 Drury Lane, London WC2B 5SW, 01–833–2181.
  *SCOTTISH ASSOCIATION OF CITIZENS' ADVICE BUREAUX*, 82 Nicolson Street, Edinburgh, 031–667–0156. See also telephone book for local provincial branches.

*NATIONAL ASSOCIATION FOR WIDOWS*, Stafford District Council Centre, Chell Road, Stafford ST1 2QA, 0785–45465. Advice, leaflets, campaigning, country wide network.

*NATIONAL BENEVOLENT FUND FOR THE AGED*, 35 New Broad Street, London EC2M 1NH, 01–638–2281/2026. A charity.

*PROFESSIONAL CLASSES AID COUNCIL*, 10 St Christopher Place, London W1M 6HY, 01–935–0641. Grants, advice and help.

*ROYAL SOCIETY FOR THE RELIEF OF INDIGENT GENTLE-WOMEN OF SCOTLAND*, 14 Rutland Square, Edinburgh EH12 2BD, 031–229–2306. A charity.

*ROYAL UNITED KINGDOM BENEFICENT ASSOCIATION*, 13 Bedford Street, The Strand, London WC2, 01–836–2575. Annuities and housing.

*SALVATION ARMY*, 280 Mare Street, London E8 1HE,

01–985–1181. Worldwide network of helpers engaged in a vast range of social work.

*SAMARITANS*, 17 Uxbridge Road, Slough SL1 1SN, 0753–32713, and 39 Walbrook, London EC4, 01–283–3400. Telephone line for the distressed.

*SOCIETY FOR THE ASSISTANCE OF LADIES IN REDUCED CIRCUMSTANCES*, Lancaster House, Malvern, Worcs, 06845–4645. A charity.

*WELLSPRING*, 2 Lord Russell Place, Edinburgh, 031–668–1131. Therapy classes and counselling. Classes in Assertiveness Training.

*WOMEN'S RIGHTS CENTRE,* North Kensington Law Centre, 74 Golbourne Road, London W10, 01–969–7473. Legal advice.

# Housing

*ABBEYFIELD SOCIETY*, 186–192 Darkes Lane, Potters Bar, Herts EN6 1AB, 0707–44845/43371. Retirement housing.

*ASSOCIATION OF HOUSING AID*, c/o Brent Housing Centre, Robert Owen House, 192 High Road, London NW10, 01–451–0911. For all kinds of housing problems.

*SELF-HELP HOUSING RESOURCE LIBRARY*, Polytechnic of North London, Ladbrooke House, Highbury Grove, N5, 01–607–2789 ext 5029. Good source of information about housing problems.

*CHAR*, a housing campaign for single people, 5–15 Crome Street, London WC1 8LS, 01–833–2071.

*HANOVER HOUSING*, 12 Ormonde Avenue, Rochford, Essex, 0772–548257 and 36 Albany St, Edinburgh, 031–557–0598.

*HELP THE AGED*, 32 Dover Street, London, 01–499–0972.

*HOUSING CENTRE TRUST*, 62 Chandos Place, London, 01–249–3424.

*INDUSTRIAL DWELLING SOCIETY*, 5th Floor, Oakway House, Stamford Hill, London N16 5SR, 01–800–9606. Housing at fair rents.

*OVER 40 ASSOCIATION FOR WOMEN WORKERS*, Mary George House, 120–122 Cromwell Road, London SW7, 01–370–2556 and 370–2545. Helps with housing problems.

*OVER 50 HOUSING ASSOCIATION*, 43 Cadogan Place, London SW7, 01–235–7536. A charity providing housing for people over 50. Accommodation in bed sitters or flatlets with meals provided.

*NATIONAL CYRENIANS*, 13 Wincheap, Canterbury, Kent, 0227-51641. Leaflets on tenants' rights and the rights of the homeless.

*SCOTS GROUP*, West End Coordinating Voluntary Services, 1 Caledonian Road, London N1 3DX, 01-833-0555/6. Young people's housing problems.

*SCOTTISH INTERMEDIATE TREATMENT CENTRE*, 19 Elmbank Street, Glasgow G7 4PB, 041-204-0417. Leaflets, information and advice for the young, particularly on housing.

*SHELTER*, 88 Old Street, London EC1V 9AX, 01–253–0202.

*WEST END OF LONDON COORDINATED VOLUNTARY SERVICES FOR HOMELESS SINGLE PEOPLE*, 3 Caledonian Road, London N1 9DX, 01-833-0555/6. For housing problems of young people.

*W.R.V.S. (Women's Royal Voluntary Service)*, 17 Old Park Road, London W1Y 4AJ, 01-499-6040. Many charitable activities plus housing association.

# Stock Market Terms

The inexperienced investor is often confused by words and abbreviations used in Stock Market reports so here is a selection of a few of the more common ones;—

ORDINARY SHARES have no guaranteed income but receive a dividend which is merely a share of any profits left over after all other expenses are paid. The directors of the company decide what dividend shall be paid.

PREFERENCE SHARES means that the holders have preference for profits and income. The shares are often sold with the promise of a certain percentage yield. They also have a preference in repayment of capital if the company is wound up.

PRE-TAX PROFIT is the amount the company has left after taking out all operating costs and adjusting remaining profit to take account of other income (from non trading activities for instance) and interest from its investments.

EPS—Earnings per share in pence.

DPS—Dividend per share in pence.

COVER—number of times the dividend is covered by net profit.

NAV—Net Asset Value which is the net worth of a company divided by the number of its shares issued.

PE—Price/earnings ratio (which is the share price divided by EPS).

YIELD—gross dividend as a percentage of the share price.

A BULL is a speculator who thinks the market is going to rise. He buys in order to resell later.

A BEAR is a speculator who thinks that prices will fall. He sells a security at a certain price in order to buy again later when the price moves down.

A STAG is a speculator who applies for shares in new issues in order to make a quick profit on the price when the shares begin to be sold.

# Useful Books

*Activity and Hobby Holidays*, Dept D, English Tourist Board, 4 Bromells Road, London SW4 0BJ. £1.99 plus postage.

*Brief for the Single Person*, Scottish Council for the Single Homeless.

*Buyers' Handbook for the Single Family Home*, Steven James Lee, Van Nostrand and Reinhold.

*The Challenge of Singleness*, Partridge, Marshall, Morgan and Scott.

*Charities Digest*, published annually by the Family Welfare Association, 501–505 Kingsland Road, Dalston, London E8 4AU, 01–254–6251.

*Fair Shares—A Layman's Guide to Buying and Selling Stocks and Shares* by Simon Rose, W.H. Allen 1986.

*Gardening in Retirement*, Age Concern, England Marketing Dept., 60 Pitcairn Road, Mitcham, Surrey CR4 2LL, 01–640–5431. £1.95.

*Help, I Need Somebody*, compiled by Sally Knight, Kimpton Publishers Ltd 1980. Guide to national associations for people in need.

*How To Die Young At Ninety* and *How To Avoid Cancer*, Dr Jan de Winter, 6 New Road, Brighton, 0273–727213.

Inland Revenue Leaflets. No IR4 *Income Tax and Pensioners* No 1R4A *The Age Allowance*.

*Leaving Home*, Mark Clark and Alan Dearling, Scots Group and the Intermediate Treatment Resource Centre 1986. Available for £1 from Shelter, 157 Waterloo Road, London SE1 8XF, 01–633–9377.

*Living With Loss*, Liz McNeill Taylor, Fontana 1983. £1.95.

*Money Observer*, 120–126 Lavender Avenue, Mitcham, Surrey CR4 3HP. £1.85.

*One is Fun!*, Delia Smith, Hodder.

*Safety First Investments* booklet from Pointon York, The Crescent, King Street, Leicester LE1 6RX, 0533–547545. £1.

*Single People Need Homes*, Council for the Single Homeless, Northern Ireland.

*Social Trends*, Central Statistical Office, 1986 edition, HMSO.

*'Someone To Talk To' Directory*, Mental Health Foundation and Routledge & Kegan Paul, £20.

*Survival Guide for Widows*, June Hemer and Ann Stanyer. Age Concern, 1986. £3.50.

*Unit Trust Year Book*, annual publication by Financial Times, Bracken House, 10 Cannon Street, London EC4P 4BY, 01–248–8000.

*Voluntary Organisations. An NCVO Directory*, Bedford Square Press/NCVO National Council for Voluntary Organisations). 1985/6.

*What To Do In An Emergency*, Reader's Digest, 25 Berkeley Square, London W1X 6AB. £13.95. Deals with a wide range of topics including legal, financial, accidents and household emergencies like gas leaks.

*Which Book of Tax*, Consumers' Association, PO Box 44, Hertford.

*Work After Work*, Lord Ezra, Quiller Press. £3.95. Lists of openings for voluntary activity for the retired. Available from REACH, 89 Southwark Street, London SE1.

*Your Rights for Pensioners*, Age Concern, England Marketing Dept., 60 Pitcairn Road, Mitcham, Surrey CR4 2LL. 90p.

*Your Tax and Savings in Retirement*, Age Concern as above.

# Source Books

Bowskill, Derek, *People Need People*, Wildwood House, London 1977.

Cruz, Nicky, *Lonely But Never Alone*, Pickering and Inglis, London 1981.

Gibson, Joan, *Open The Door*, Gateway, Bath 1984.

Hulme, William Edward, *Creative Loneliness*, Lakeland, London 1979.

Jerrome, Dorothy, *Women and Loneliness*, Hastings Women's Study Group and Dorothy Jerrome 1984.

Kurtz, Irma, *Loneliness*, Basil Blackwell, Oxford 1983.

Peplau, Letitia Anne and Perlman, Daniel, *Loneliness, A Source Book of Current Theory, Research and Therapy*. Chichester, New York 1982.

Schultz, Terri, *Bittersweet—Surviving and Growing from Loneliness* Thos V. Cromwell and Co, New York 1976; Penguin 1978.

Smith, Blanche Marie, *Single Women of Today, problems and adjustments*, Greenwood Press, London.

Trevivian, Roy, *So You're Lonely?* Fount 1978.

# Index